LIVING TO 120 AND
BEYOND

WHERE SCIENCE AND SPIRIT MEET

DR. EDMUND CHEIN , MD , JD

LIVING TO 120 AND BEYOND
Where Science and Spirit Meet

iUniverse books may be ordered through booksellers or by contacting:

iUniverse
1663 Liberty Drive
Bloomington, IN 47403
www.iuniverse.com
1-800-Authors (1-800-288-4677)

Because of the dynamic nature of the Internet, any web
addresses or links contained in this book may have changed
since publication and may no longer be valid.

ISBN: 978-1-4759-9398-1 (sc)
ISBN: 978-1-4759-9399-8 (e)

Library of Congress Control Number: 2013912210

Print information available on the last page.

iUniverse rev. date: 03/22/2017

CONTENTS

Preface ix

Introduction... xi

Maintaining Good Health and Achieving Longevity:
Medical, Scientific, and Medical-Technology Approaches

1. A Long Life—God's Promise 1
   - Overview 1
   - Demystifying the Promise of "120 Years".......................1
   - How Do We Each Fulfill the Promise of
     Living 120 Years?..4
   - Chronology versus Biology 5
   - Cellular Code Defined and Described.............................5
     - Chromosomes and DNA..5
     - Telomeres and Telomerase.......................................6
2. Telomeres and Telomerase: How They Impact
   Longevity and Lasting Good Health 9
   - Overview 9
   - History of Telomere and Telomerase Research 10
     - Timeline of Telomere and Telomerase
       Breakthroughs 10
   - The Roles of Telomeres and Telomerase
     in Attaining the Full Life Span of 120 12
     - Medical Studies That Support the Benefits of
       Telomerase Activation......................................15
   - Hormone Replenishment: The Key Ingredient
     to Longevity..17
     - Total Hormone Supplementation............................18

3. The Telomere Yardstick:
   Three Separate Studies of Biological Age 21
      Overview 21
      Biological Age by the Numbers 22
      Individual Patient Results 23
      The Program Defined 31
         Key Hormones 31
         Key Nutrients 32
4. Which Bioidentical Hormones Are Related to
   Your Stem Cells in Regeneration and Rejuvenation? 35
      Overview 35
      What Are Stem Cells? 36
         Stem Cells Defined 36
         The Basics of Stem-Cell Therapy 36
         Essential Hormones in Stem-Cell Therapy 37
      The Role of Bio-identical Hormones and
         Growth Factors in Stem Cells 38
         IGF-1, HGH, and other Growth Factors. 38
         Estrogen and Pregnenolone Influence
           the Quantity and Quality of the Stem
           Cells in Our Bodies 41
         Thyroid Hormones and Melatonin Hormone
           Also Influence the Quantity and Quality
           of Our Stem Cells 42
5. The Method and Medical Technology of the 21st
   Century—How to Reverse Biological Age, Attain
   Better Health, and Increase the Life Span[1] 43
      Overview 43
      Reversing Biological Age, Attaining Better Health,
         and Increasing the Life Span 44
         The Method Defined and Described 44
      Checking and Assessing Hormone Levels 45
      Tests Needed for Telomerase Activation
         Therapy—Women 47
      Tests Needed for Telomerase Activation
         Therapy—Men 49

Why Telomeres Are Important......................................52
   Telomere Length and Its Significance...................53
   Telomere Length's Impact on Biological Age 54
   Understanding Biological Age versus
      Chronological Age...55
Telomere Analysis 56
   Test Procedures and Protocols: TAT,
      HT Q-FISH, PCR 57
   Why TAT Is Optimal 59
   Follow-up 59

6. The Delicate Balance of a Strong Body—
The Difference between Hormone Supplementation
and Nutrition/Exercise 61
   Overview 61
   Telomere Length and Good Health 62
      Hormones and Telomere Length............................63
      Nutrients and Telomere Length..............................65
   Addition, Not Subtraction—Hormone
      Supplementation Used to Enhance Diet
      and Exercise Plans 67
      Fitness, Diet, and Exercise Gurus Who Died
      before the Age of 100 68
   Maintaining the Delicate Balance—Strength,
      Wellness, and Resiliency 73

7. Know Your Own Numbers—Tests Needed to Check
Hormone Levels and Assess Health 75
   Overview 75
   Tests Needed to Check Overall Health and
      Hormone Levels—Women....................................76
   Tests Needed to Check Overall Health and
      Hormone Levels—Men 78
   What to Expect During the Testing Phase....................81
   What to Expect While on the Program 82
   Example Health Log...83

8. Debunking the Controversy—Testosterone and
    Growth Hormone Supplementation Do Not Cause
    or Worsen Any Type of Cancer 87
        Overview 87
        Testosterone Supplementation—Facts versus
            Myths 88
        Growth Hormone (IGF and HGH)
            Supplementation—Facts versus Myths 89
9. The Difference between Wisdom and Knowledge—
    What Western Physicians May or May Not Know 95
        Overview 95
        Knowledge: The Benefits and Limitations of
            Western Medicine 96
        Wisdom: There Is No Substitute for Treating
            the Body as a Whole...97
        "Why Don't My Doctors Know All This?" 98
        Integrating Knowledge and Wisdom for
            Better Balance 103
10. How to Stay Healthy Living on a Poisoned Planet—
    The Polluted Environment We Have Created 105
        Overview 105
        The Risk of Heavy Metals 106
            Arsenic, Uranium, Barium, Thallium, Antimony.....107
            Health Tests to Check Levels of Heavy
                Metals in Humans..110
            Treatment for Heavy-Metal Poisoning 112
        How Environmental Factors Impact Health and
            Longevity—And What to Do to Protect
            Ourselves..113
            Solvents, Cleansers, Pesticides, Plastics
                Bottles/Containers, Detergents, and
                Skin/Body Care Products.............................113
        The Dangers of Mold and Mildew 115
Essentials for Health, Wellness, and Longevity........................123
        Key Points to Remember 123

A Word from the Author 133

My Pledge to God 135

Conclusion 137

References and Resources 139

      Websites 139

      Books 139

      Articles 141

      Research Studies 147

About Edmund Chein, MD, JD 149

Notes 151

A wise man should consider that health is the greatest of human blessings.

—Hippocrates

PREFACE

As of this writing, my chronological age is 61, but my estimated biological age by telomere length measurement is 33.9.* The patients who follow my advice have no regrets, and they thrive as a result of my recommendations. Health and longevity can only be achieved by treating the body as a whole, honoring its wisdom and focusing on systemic care, rather than depending on reactive responses to disease. Monitoring hormone levels and replenishing them as needed are key to the modality I recommend, in addition to vitamin and nutrient supplements (vitamin B_{12}, folate, vitamin B_3, vitamins C, D, and E, magnesium, zinc, and essential fatty acids like omega-3).† Hormones play a key role in activating telomerase, which in turn elongates the telomere portion of our DNA. Telomere length keeps cells healthy and vital, and achieving such health and vitality is the ultimate goal of antiaging and longevity.

In 2009, the Nobel Prize in Medicine was awarded to three scientists (Elizabeth Blackburn, Carol Greider, and Jack Szostak)

---

*   We will explain telomere length measurement and its impact on health and longevity throughout the chapters of this book.

†   Throughout this book, descriptions of hormone replenishment/ supplementation therapy and diet/nutrition supplementation refer to therapies and modalities administered by a medical professional and accompanied by appropriate monitoring on a regular basis. The information, ideas, and suggestions in this book are not intended as a substitute for professional medical advice or professional mental health advice. Before following any suggestions contained in this book, you should consult your personal physician and/or personal mental health professional.

working in telomere and telomerase research, just as I do. Such like-minded physicians and scientists and I have made progress in that area of research as well, both before and since that time. In addition to Drs. Blackburn, Greider, and Szostak, I wish to acknowledge the work of Drs. Boggess, Brouillette, Kaszubowska, Sanchez, Sheppard, Williams, and Xu, as well as all their teams, for their respective work related to telomeres, telomerase, multivitamins, hormones, etc. Many thanks to all of them; their findings support and validate mine.

I wrote this book in order to increase general awareness of my recommended medical method for achieving lasting good health and longevity, including the technology used to employ this method. Please read the introduction, which will explain some of these concepts and terms in greater detail, providing a foundation for a more informed reading of the medical and scientific text contained in this book.

Wishing all readers lasting good health and increased longevity! Many thanks for reading this book.

—Edmund Chein, MD, JD

Edmund Chein, MD, JD, *is an expert on health and longevity. He currently runs the Palm Springs Life Extension Institute, holds a US patent for Total Hormone Replacement Therapy, and is the author of* Age Reversal: From Hormones to Telomerase; Bio-Identical Hormones and Telomerase: The Nobel Prize-Winning Research into Human Life Extension and Health; *and numerous other publications.*

INTRODUCTION

Modern medical modalities and technology allow us to reverse our biological age, thereby extending our life span to at least 120, the age God promised us in Genesis 6:3. If this seems a statement better suited to religion than biology, consider the Nobel Prize in Medicine awarded in 2009. Drs. Blackburn, Greider, and Szostak—the three scientists who received this award—did so because of their research in telomeres and telomerase: simply by supplying telomerase to cellular DNA, physicians and scientists can keep the cells alive forever.

Granted, the technology necessary to introduce the telomerase directly into the human body (as opposed to the cells in a laboratory environment) is many years away. However, the technology that allows scientists to safely use bioidentical hormones to activate and optimize the levels of hormones in the body is already available. Many hormones activate and increase telomerase in our cells. Thus, by keeping some of those hormones at optimal levels, we can regenerate and rejuvenate our aging cells, thereby reversing our biological age. If we can reverse our biological age in this manner, attaining the chronological age of 120 becomes a realistic expectation, not merely a scriptural promise rarely fulfilled.

This may sound too good to be true, but it isn't. It is simply a biological fact. As we explore telomeres, telomerase, and hormones further, the beauty and simplicity of our human makeup will be revealed. For now, suffice it to say that each individual's DNA is unique in the history of the universe. Never before was there a creature with our individual DNA, and after we each die, there will never be another creature with our individual DNA, either. This is the science behind law enforcement's use of DNA evidence in criminal forensics. As far as longevity, health, and wellness are concerned, 120 years is our birthright, by means of God's promise to us. He put each one of us on this planet for a purpose, complete with that promise of a 120-year life span, so if we don't make it to 120, it is because we have neglected our bodies and our health.

At this time in human history, we are more intelligent and more useful to society than any prior generation, including our parents' and grandparents' generations. That means God's intention for us to fulfill our purpose is even stronger, and therefore the promise to attain 120 years is that much more likely. Any of us who believe this must also believe that we owe it to ourselves to cultivate good health and to maintain our bodies as the "temples" God designed.

The medical modality and technology that will be revealed throughout the pages of this book will enable each of us to reach 120 years—not just that life span in chronological years, but in continued good health, with no age-related diseases or infirmities, and with vitality, functionality, and activity until the end of life.

Now let's embark on the exciting adventure of cultivating and maintaining good health, attaining longevity with a sustained high quality of life, and living with the enduring positive spirit of true and complete well-being that will last throughout the life span.

[* All names of individuals described have been changed or eliminated in order to protect their privacy.]

Maintaining Good Health
and Achieving Longevity:
Medical, Scientific, and
Medical-Technology Approaches

1

A LONG LIFE——GOD'S PROMISE

No longer will people be considered old at 100! Only
the cursed will die that young!

—Isaiah 65:20

Overview

This chapter will define some of the basics of our cellular code, including chromosomes, DNA, telomeres, and telomerase. Many of the concepts and terminology outlined here will be described in greater detail in subsequent chapters, most notably telomeres and telomerase. The foundational concepts and terminology discussed in this chapter will provide a more informed reading of the rest of the book.

In addition, we will discuss God's promise of a 120-year life span, as described in Genesis 6:3. This book will explore the spiritual component of good health and well-being, to which the body-mind-spirit connection will testify.

Demystifying the Promise of "120 Years"

According to the Bible, before the flood of Noah, many people lived longer than the 120 years that God later promised. Adam lived 930 years. The longest-lived human in the Bible was Methuselah, who lived 969 years (according to Genesis 5:27).

The Bible doesn't tell us why the life span was so long at first. This is not a religious or philosophical book, so our intent here is not to engage in scriptural exegesis, but we must have a brief discussion of Scripture in order to understand the meaning and intent of the promised 120 years, as well as the earlier biblical 900-plus-year life spans. In practical and scientific terms, perhaps these life spans allowed for faster population growth. There were fewer people on earth, and in order to have larger families, every individual would naturally have had to live longer. Longer life spans also would have allowed knowledge to be preserved in memory and the oral tradition, as writing had not yet been invented. In societies with no written records, the death of an elder would have been equivalent to the loss of an entire physical library or electronic database in contemporary society.

Nevertheless, although Noah himself lived to be 950, during Noah's time God declared an end to these long life spans: "Then the Lord said, 'My Spirit shall not abide in man forever, for he is flesh, but his days shall be 120 years'" (Gen. 6:3). Today, the Guinness world record age for humans is a couple of years beyond that 120-year mark, just as God promised in Genesis. (To be precise, the oldest human documented since the time of Noah was Jeanne Calment of France, who was 122 years, 164 days old at the time of her death.)

Some scholars suggest that the 120 years referred to the time that would pass before the flood took place. However, God made that decision *after* Noah reached the age of 500 years in Genesis 5:32. In fact, Noah was already 600 years old when the floodwaters covered the earth, according to Genesis 7:6. Therefore, the flood occurred within 100 years of God's decision. So if the 120 years was not a reference to the time that passed prior to the flood, it must have been a reference to man's actual life span.

Many read Genesis 6:3 and expect that God would have implemented the change in life span at that time. However, as we read further, we see that people continued to live much longer than 120 years, even during the time that followed the flood. (This included Noah himself, who died at 950, as mentioned above.) Some consider this an obvious contradiction in the Bible, but, in fact, God did not say that the shortening of the life span would be immediate. The life span did gradually decline after God's decision to limit man's time on earth. Jacob, the father of Israel, became the last person in the Bible to live beyond 120 years.

From a biblical perspective, the long life span that God gave man before the flood allowed humans too much time for wickedness. By shortening the life span to 120 years, God helped man lessen the evil of which individuals are capable by reducing the number of years available for committing acts of evil. In addition, God viewed our bodies as "his temple in which the holy spirit lives" (1 Cor. 6:19). Shortening the life span to 120 years made it easier for humans to maintain their individual "temples," as the ever-increasing population on earth required more and more natural resources for its ongoing development and sustenance. Thus, we realize that depletion of natural resources was always an issue; God is just far wiser than we are. Perhaps the Bible has actually foretold the state of our present environment, as well as our medical advances! Only time will tell.

> If God intended for us to live to age 120, at age 60 we should be in our prime. We should not have any age-related diseases or infirmities, even at 70, 80, or 90!

3

How Do We Each Fulfill the Promise of Living 120 Years?

Let's move beyond the biblical and theoretical to the scientific and practical. We can hold God to his promise of 120 years if we do our job of checking and maintaining the "temple" he gave each of us. By "temple," of course, I mean our individual bodies. In other words, if God intended for us to live to age 120, at age 60 we should be in our prime. We should not have any age-related diseases or infirmities, even at 70, 80, or 90! With five or fewer decades to live until the end of our promised life span, we should be vibrant and vital. However, like a car designed to run 100,000 miles, our bodies must be checked, cared for, and maintained in order to operate properly until that limit is reached. The reason we prematurely suffer age-related diseases and die earlier than 120 is simply that we neglect our bodies, the temples God gave each of us.

Let me immediately clarify that last statement, because many of us do not neglect our bodies in terms of what contemporary medicine and consumer health advises. But most of us do neglect what is required if we seek to attain our promised 120-year life span and to do so with vitality and vibrancy throughout it. Simply put, we each must check within our own bodily systems that which "regular" (allopathic) doctors often miss. This includes deficiencies in hormones, vitamins, minerals, essential amino acids, and essential fatty acids. It also includes food allergies and sensitivities, as well as the presence of environmental metal and chemical toxicities. (These toxicities did not exist when God created the earth; God did not create pesticides or phthalates from plastics.) From among all these, hormones are the most important, as evidenced by the 2009 Nobel Prize in Medicine, awarded to three doctors for their telomere and telomerase research (as mentioned in the preface and introduction). However, that does not minimize the importance of vitamins and nutrients. As we explore these topics further, we will see the importance of each individual component, along with the significance of their interrelationships vis-à-vis lasting good health and increased longevity.

Chronology versus Biology

We have already established our goal of attaining God's promised life span of 120 years. But there's not much point to achieving the chronological age of 120 unless we maintain our good health and vitality. In order to do that, we must keep our biological age as low as possible so that when we reach the chronological age of 120, we will be far younger biologically. As the popular phrasing goes, we must make "80 the new 60." To use myself as an example, as stated in the preface, my chronological age is currently 61, but biologically I am only 33.9. The technology necessary to achieve this difference between chronological versus biological age resides in our own DNA. Thus, before we take our discussion any further, let's define and describe telomeres, telomerase, hormones, and the connection between them.

> We must make 80 the new 60!

Cellular Code Defined and Described

Chromosomes and DNA

Chromosomes are highly condensed rods of deoxyribonucleic acid (DNA), the genetic material containing the building blocks of life. As we've already discussed, every individual's DNA is unique. Our DNA holds a specific code of biological and physiological instructions. In short, our DNA tells our bodies how and when to grow, develop, and function. These instructions are organized into units called genes. The chromosomes themselves serve as the storage centers for this essential material, and they periodically divide along with the cells, replicating to make copies of their component DNA. Chromosomes also play a key role in sexual reproduction, because they allow organisms to pass on their genetic material to their descendants.

Organisms with cell nuclei, such as humans and all higher life forms, have chromosomes inside each cell nucleus. These chromosomes usually come in pairs, with each cell retaining its chromosomes in diploid form (meaning that it is a complete set). During sexual reproduction, each cell receives only half of the parent organism's genetic material, stored in haploid form (meaning that the parent has passed down half its genes).

Telomeres and Telomerase

Telomeres are protective structures at the ends of our chromosomes. The primary function of telomeres is to preserve chromosomal integrity and prevent DNA degradation. We can think of telomeres as "caps" of a sort. As such, telomeres are essential to the optimal functionality, viability, and vitality of cells. However, telomeres shorten every time a human cell divides, so every human's biological age is closely associated with the length of that individual's telomeres.

Telomerase is an enzyme capable of maintaining telomeres and repairing short telomeres by elongating them to regain their optimal length. Thus, telomerase can add telomeric repeats to chromosome ends. Pathologically, it plays a key role in such conditions as cancer, because it sustains the ongoing growth of cancer cells. Healthy (nonpathological) cells usually produce little to no telomerase, which is why healthy cells progressively shorten their telomeres in successive cycles of cell division. As a result, these cells eventually reach a critically short length that triggers cell death or an irreversible cellular "arrest" called replicative senescence. This is better known as "old age," with all its attendant diseases and infirmities.

In other words, because telomeres shorten every time a human cell divides, the length of an individual's telomeres is closely associated with his or her biological age. Telomere length can be used as a molecular marker to measure the degree of an organism's aging and to estimate the biological age of that organism (i.e., each individual human). Thus, just as we saw above how telomeres and telomerase are essential to studying and treating cancer, so are they equally essential to studying longevity and to developing the technology and modalities necessary to cultivating and maintaining health and wellness across the life span and into chronological senescence. Much research has shown that the control of telomere length has the potential to treat many diseases associated with aging,[1] thereby allowing humans to appear physiologically/biologically young, to attain the God-promised age of 120, and to live beyond the observed maximum human life span of 122 years. (We will explore this in greater detail in chapter 5, when we discuss the method and technology needed to extend the life span while simultaneously establishing and maintaining optimal health.)

In the next chapter, we will further explore the study and research of telomeres and telomerase, and the ways in which they (as well as hormone levels) positively affect good health, well-being, and attainment of the full life span.

2

TELOMERES AND TELOMERASE: HOW THEY IMPACT LONGEVITY AND LASTING GOOD HEALTH

May you live all the days of your life.

—Jonathan Swift

Overview

This chapter will expand our discussion of telomeres and telomerase, further illustrating their essential roles in achieving longevity and attaining/maintaining good health. We will also discuss the importance of hormones and hormone replenishment/supplementation therapy as a key component of our recommended longevity program.

Please be aware that we will discuss the importance of telomeres, telomerase, and hormones throughout this book in order to emphasize—and reemphasize—just how key they are to successfully attaining and maintaining good health and well-being, and to achieving the full life span with an attendant sound body and mind.

And now, because telomeres and telomerase will likely be little-known topics to most, let's explore the history of their scientific discovery and application.

History of Telomere and Telomerase Research

To briefly review, telomeres are cap-like structures at the end of our chromosomes that shorten every time a human cell divides. The length of every individual's telomeres is closely associated with his or her biological age. Research has suggested that controlling telomere length has the potential to treat many diseases associated with aging, thereby allowing humans to live physiologically and biologically "younger"—that is, with increased vitality and vibrancy, and in better health—and to attain a chronological age that is beyond the observed maximum human life span of 122 years.

The initial discovery of the telomere occurred in 1938. Almost 60 years later (in 1997), scientists first cloned telomerase, the enzyme responsible for telomere maintenance and repair. Let's further examine the research completed between the discovery of telomeres and the first cloning of telomerase, as well as the vast amount of research completed since 1997—including the 2009 Nobel Prize in Medicine, which was awarded for telomere and telomerase research.

Timeline of Telomere and Telomerase Breakthroughs

In 1938, geneticist Herman Muller[1] first discovered and named telomeres in the fruit fly when observing structures that served as protective caps on the chromosomes' ends, preventing DNA damage. Two years later, geneticist Barbara McClintock[2] discovered that without telomeres, chromosomes would fuse to each other, causing cell death. However, neither Muller nor

McClintock realized that telomere shortening was associated with human aging.

The nature of telomere shortening was first proposed by Soviet scientist Alexei Olovnikov and American scientist James Watson, in 1971 and 1972, respectively.[3] Both scientists realized that every cell replication must result in a loss of some DNA. Olovnikov was the first to posit that telomere shortening was the mechanism that limited the number of times a cell could divide.

In 1975, Elizabeth Blackburn (Yale University) and Jack Szostak (Harvard Medical School) discovered that yeast cells were able to re-elongate their telomeres.[4] They theorized that the yeast's telomeres were lengthened by an enzyme that would later be named telomerase. In 1984, Blackburn and one of her students, Carol Greider, isolated telomerase.[5] (As previously mentioned, in 2009, Blackburn, Greider, and Szostak were awarded the Nobel Prize in Medicine for their work in discovering the structure and mechanism of telomeres and telomerase.[6])

In 1998, a team at Texas University Southwest Medical School added the gene for telomerase to normal human cells by means of a plasmid, creating a line of cells that were able to divide indefinitely.[7] (A plasmid is an extrachrosomal ring of DNA; plasmids replicate autonomously and are most typically found in bacteria.) This first-time cloning of telomerase demonstrated that normal human cells can be made immortal.

In 2003, a team led by Richard Cawthorn at the Utah State University studied 143 individuals over the age of 60 who had donated their blood between 1982 and 1986 (20 years prior), measuring the telomere length in their blood cells. They found that the mortality rate of those individuals with shorter telomeres was nearly twice as high as that of individuals with longer telomeres.[8] This provided solid evidence of correlation between telomere shortening and death from old age or age-related diseases in humans.

In 2008, scientists led by Dr. Maria Blasco at the National Center for Biotechnology in Spain created a line of mice whose cells had been engineered to produce more telomerase than normal mice. This allowed these genetically engineered mice to live an average of 138 percent longer than normal mice.[9] Furthermore, these mice stayed healthier and more athletic for a longer time. This represented the first time that the life span of a multicellular mammal had ever been extended, and the quality of life improved, through telomere lengthening therapy.

> The therapeutic modality and medical method recommended in this book are not known to increase cancer risk.

The Roles of Telomeres and Telomerase in Attaining the Full Life Span of 120

Telomere length is one of the best indicators of aging. This is true of any organism at any age, including humans, and it is the reason why telomere length is such an effective way to estimate the biological age.

To take this a step further, we need to understand that all humans do not have telomeres of ideal length—if we did, we would all live to 120 . . . or longer. Telomeres shorten (erode progressively, to use more scientific terminology) as a result of cumulative cycles of cell regeneration over the course of an organism's lifetime. That is, telomeres become shorter as we age. Therefore, lengthening our telomeres is the most effective way to live longer and in better health. The best way to lengthen telomeres is to activate telomerase, the enzyme that maintains and repairs them (see "Hormone Replenishment: The Key Ingredient to Longevity," below).

However, in addition to enabling longevity, telomeres and telomerase play a significant role in cancer biology. More than 95 percent of all types of malignant tumors activate telomerase during their formation; as a result, telomerase is considered necessary to sustain cancer growth. Scientists have begun clinical trials and tests exploring ways to inhibit telomerase activity, and breakthroughs are likely to be forthcoming. This is important information to know, but even more important is our understanding that the therapeutic modality and medical method recommended in this book are not known to increase cancer risk. (We will explore the actual method in greater detail in chapter 5.)

Medical studies continue to show that short telomeres are responsible for causing aging, as well as age-related disease and debilitation. Without telomerase repair, critically short telomeres can—and will—severely harm the cell, often causing permanent damage. Because every cell has telomeres capping the ends of the chromosomes in its nucleus, it's essential to determine telomere length. A majority of short telomeres in an individual will result in premature aging, disease (particularly a greater risk of developing problems with the cardiovascular and central nervous systems), and failure to attain the full life span.

Of course, lifestyle and genetics are also key factors that contribute to aging and disease. And, not surprisingly, obesity, smoking, psychological and emotional stress, and other unhealthy states of being and habitual behaviors all contribute to telomere shortening. These behaviors and states increase physical stress, harm the immune system, and create inflammations—factors all known to contribute to decreased well-being and shorter life spans. Conversely, diet (nutrition and supplementation), exercise, and sleep all can decrease the effects of stress, strengthen the immune system, reduce the amount of inflammations in the body, and inhibit telomere shortening.

> A majority of short telomeres in an individual will result in premature aging, disease, and failure to attain the full life span.

To underscore its importance, let's reemphasize that healthy diet (with appropriate supplementation); regular exercise (appropriate for existing health conditions); sufficient sleep (seven to nine hours a night); and positive supporting habits (meditation, yoga, breathing exercises, and journaling). All of these will encourage better health—to a great extent by limiting telomere shortening. Thus, by promoting telomere lengthening through telomerase activation, we can further improve these results. (Again, we will explore the method in greater detail in chapter 5).

As the foregoing clearly shows, telomeres are the key to longevity—to attaining the full life span of 120. It's as simple as that.

Now let's review the medical and scientific data that supports this groundbreaking—and potentially life-changing—information.

> Healthy diet, sufficient sleep, regular exercise, and other positive supporting habits all will encourage better health—to a great extent, by limiting telomere shortening.

Medical Studies That Support the Benefits of Telomerase Activation

As stated above, there had been some speculation within the medical/scientific community that lengthening telomeres in normal human cells could potentially increase the risk of cancer. However, studies over the last ten years have consistently refuted these doubts. Several publications by Jerry Shay and Wooding Wright at the University of Texas Southwest Medical Center, as well as Calvin Harley, who reviewed 86 publications on the relationship between telomerase and cancer, concluded that (1) telomerase was not a cancer-causing oncogene, and (2) telomerase did not cause cells to lose growth control and become cancerous.[10]

In 2001, Drs. Keith Williams and Kimberly Boggess at the University of North Carolina demonstrated that progesterone (not progestin or medroxy-progesterone) inhibits endometrial telomerase.[11] (The findings and conclusions of Drs. Williams and Boggess validated my own long-standing position that progesterone prevents breast, uterine, and prostate cancers.)

In 2005, Dr. Gomez Sanchez and his group at La Paz University in Spain showed that the growth hormone directly activates telomerase.[12] Also in 2005, Dr. Michael Sheppard affirmed, "Growth hormone therapy *does not* induce cancer."[13] Again in 2005, the California—based biotech company Geron discovered and patented TA-65, a telomerase activator. (The New York-based supplement company T.A. Sciences manufactures TA-65, which is made from the Chinese herb *Astragalus membranaceus.**)

---

*   Noel Patton, founder and CEO of T.A. Sciences, has been taking TA-65 since 2008. His chronological age is 66 (at the time of this writing). He claimed to have performed telomere tests on his own DNA but declined to share the test results. The journal *Rejuvenation*

In 2007, Dr. Scott Brouillette and his group in Scotland demonstrated that telomere length is a predictor of the onset of coronary disease.[14]

In 2008, Dr. L. Kaszubowska at the University of Gdnask in Poland showed that centenarians have long telomeres in their lymphocytes (cells of the lymphatic system, most notably white blood cells).[15] (Dr. Kaszubowska's findings and conclusions proved my own long-held position that lengthening telomeres *does not* cause cancer.)

In 2009, a joint study by Georgetown University and the National Cancer Institute concluded that short telomeres lead to chromosome instabilities, which in turn lead to cancer.[16] Also in 2009, Dr. H. Xu and his group at the National Human Genome Research Institute (part of the National Institutes of Health [NIH]) demonstrated that the use of multivitamins is associated with longer telomere length among women.[17] Needless to say, the most significant achievement of 2009 was the already mentioned awarding of the Nobel Prize in Medicine to Drs. Blackburn, Greider, and Szostak for their telomere and telomerase research.[18]

In July 2010, an international team of scientists compared telomere length with incidences of cancer in 787 patients, finding that those patients who had short telomeres had three times the incidence of cancer as patients with long telomeres. These researchers suggested that keeping telomeres at their optimal length through telomerase activation could likely prevent cancer.[19]

During this time frame, Dr. Maria Blasco continued her studies on mice. A prolific scientist who heads the Telomeres and

---

Research (February 2011, 45-56)cited studies following T.A. Sciences customers taking TA-65, along with vitamin supplements. These subjects' mean telomere length did not increase.

Telomerase Group at the Spanish National Cancer Research Centre, Dr. Blasco concluded that in the group of genetically engineered mice studied, TA-65 rescued cells in jeopardy and improved health without increasing cancer incidence (a risk when cells can divide for longer periods of time). In her study, a group of middle-aged and old mice ate food enhanced with TA-65, while the control group ate plain food. After three months, Blasco's team took blood samples from both groups in order to measure telomere length. Sure enough, the mice that ingested the TA-65 had a lower percentage of "very short telomeres." However, the changes did not last, overall longevity did not change, and average telomere length of the treated mice did not change.[20]

Hormone replenishment is the most effective way to activate telomerase—and thereby to achieve long life and lasting good health.

Hormone Replenishment: The Key Ingredient to Longevity

As the collective research above clearly shows, telomere length is directly linked to longevity. By activating telomerase, as we've seen, we can increase the life span with attendant good health. However, telomerase will not be available for use for several years (at least), and products like TA-65 have not proved consistently effective. Consequently, scientists and medical researchers have sought methods to stimulate telomerase activation—that is, "turn on" telomerase in the cells in order to maintain and repair telomeres. Through this study and research, they discovered that hormones positively impact telomerase. Therefore, hormone replenishment is currently the most effective way to activate telomerase.

Because hormone balancing (replenishment/supplementation) therapy has proved—and continues to prove—quite successful in improving age-related diseases and reversing biological age, I too studied and researched it extensively. Following the findings of the collective studies and research summarized above, as well as my own research, I embarked on developing an effective anti-aging/longevity modality. (Again, we will discuss the actual modality and medical method in greater detail in chapter 5).

Total Hormone Supplementation

After developing a unique and effective program, I obtained a US patent for Total Hormone Supplementation/Replacement Therapy in 1999. The patent's abstract (encapsulated below) describes the salient features of this anti-aging modality/program:

> A hormone replenishment method particularly useful in maintaining the body's neuroendocrine clock at optimal levels and combating conditions associated with advancing age is disclosed. The method includes determining that the level of human growth hormone and at least two other supplemental hormones are below optimal or predetermined physiological levels for an adult human. Once it has been established that the level of human growth hormone and at least two other supplemental hormones are below predetermined physiological levels, the method includes establishing a regimen of replenishment of the level of the deficient hormones to optimal or predetermined physiological levels. The supplements include the sex hormones, namely testosterone, progesterone, and estrogen, the pineal hormone melatonin, the adrenal hormones, namely DHEA and pregnenolone, the thyroid hormone, and the thymus hormone. A method of increasing life expectancy and life span by determining the level of growth hormone and at least two of the

> supplemental hormones and establishing a regimen for the maintenance of the level of human growth hormone and supplemental hormones at optimal or predetermined physiological levels is also disclosed.[21]

To condense and clarify the abstract's language, this modality/ program is basically used to replenish depleted essential human hormones; that is, below optimal physiological levels for adult humans. The end goal of this therapy, of course, is to improve health and attain the promised life span of 120. As described above in the patent abstract, the hormones assessed, and replenished when necessary, include the growth hormone, the sex hormones (testosterone, progesterone, and estrogen), the pineal hormone (melatonin), the adrenal hormones (DHEA [dehydro-epiandosterone] and pregnenolone), thyroid hormones (T3 and T4), and the thymus hormone. (Again, we will explore and explain the method in greater detail in chapter 5.)

In summary, then, optimal-length telomeres are critical to attaining and maintaining good health and to achieving the full life span—medical and scientific research have proved this time and time again, and will continue to do so. But, regrettably, every human does not have telomeres of ideal length. Telomerase activation can prevent further cellular damage and reverse biological aging, but at this time, such activation requires the continuous supplementation of hormones. (That is, appropriate hormone replenishment administered to their physiologic optimal levels and regularly monitored by a medical professional).

As our discussion thus far has clearly illustrated, telomeres, telomerase, and hormones all are critical to achieving longevity and lasting good health. Accordingly, we will explore all this in greater detail throughout the subsequent sections of this book.

> Telomeres must be of optimal length; telomerase must be activated to inhibit telomere shortening and/or promote telomere lengthening; and hormones must be balanced and replenished (through appropriate medical method) when needed.

In the next chapter, we will examine the test results of three unrelated individuals. These analyses of telomeres and hormones will allow us to fully and conclusively see their positive impact on attaining and maintaining good health and achieving the full life span.

3

THE TELOMERE YARDSTICK: THREE SEPARATE STUDIES OF BIOLOGICAL AGE

Thou shalt come to thy grave in full age, like as a shock of corn cometh in in his season.

—Job 5:26

Overview

Before we delve into the details of the recommended medical method and modality, let's study three separate individuals following the program in order to see the results that are possible. (We will explore the recommended medical technology, method, and modality in detail in chapter 5.)

This chapter will analyze the test results of these three individuals, showing the extent of the method's potential efficacy. We will also see further evidence as to the impact of telomeres, telomerase, and hormone levels on longevity and lasting good health.

Biological Age by the Numbers

We will more deeply discuss the importance of biological age in chapter 5, but for now, let's consider biological age to be an excellent indicator of general total good health and well-being. As discussed earlier, measurement of biological age is the most accurate when calculated according to the length of the telomeres in the DNA of every individual person, expressed in "the percentage of short telomeres" in a pool of cells (the lesser percentage, the younger the person). Thus, we can think of telomeres as cellular measures by which we can determine the difference between biological and chronological age for any and every human.[1]

Let's see how those measurement values vary from person to person and what telomere length can tell us about an individual's health and potential for longevity.

> Telomere length is the cellular measure of biological age.

Individual Patient Results

The tables below show the basic telomere data of three individuals* who have been on the total hormone supplementation/replacement therapy program. This hormone supplementation/replacement includes the human growth hormone (HGH).

[**NOTE:** *These three individuals are each a composite that represents three different groups of individuals who have been on the total hormone supplementation/replacement therapy, including HGH, for varying amounts of time.*]

---

* The individuals described in these composites are intended to serve as illustrations of the program; their identities have been withheld in order to protect their privacy. Actual results may vary.

SUMMARY OF RESULTS:

Chronological age (years): 57.2

Estimated biological age (years): 29.1

Percentage of short telomeres (<3Kb): 14.78

Percentile of percentage of short telomeres: 12.44

Median telomere length (Kb): 6.502

Percentile of median telomere length: 53.72

IMPORTANT

In order to carry out any longitudinal analysis of your telomere length and estimated biological age, please record the code of this report for future measurements.

CODE: USAZ003012RE

LIFE LENGTH

Results Summary—Patient Number 1 (NQ)

Sex	Female
Chronological Age (in Years)	57.2
Estimated Biological Age (in Years)	29.1
Amount of Years in Program	14.0
Percentage of Short Telomeres (<3 Kb*)	14.78
Percentile of Percentage of Short Telomeres	12.44
Median Telomere Length (Kb)	6.502
Percentile of Median Telomere Length	53.72

---

*   Kb = kilobase(s), the standard measurement value used to determine telomere length

RESULTS REPORT

SUMMARY OF RESULTS:

Chronological age (years): 60.4

Estimated biological age (years): 33.8

Percentage of short telomeres (<3Kb): 16.28

Percentile of percentage of short telomeres: 26.72

Median telomere length (Kb): 7.335

Percentile of median telomere length: 80.9

IMPORTANT

In order to carry out any longitudinal analysis of your telomere length and estimated biological age, please record the code of this report for future measurements.

CODE: USAZ003001

 LIFE LENGTH

Results Summary—Patient Number 2 (EC)

Sex	Male
Chronological Age (in Years)	60.4
Estimated Biological Age (in Years)	33.9
Amount of Years in Program	22.0
Percentage of Short Telomeres (<3 Kb)	16.28
Percentile of Percentage of Short Telomeres	26.72
Median Telomere Length (Kb)	7.335
Percentile of Median Telomere Length	80.90

RESULTS REPORT

SUMMARY OF RESULTS:

Chronological age (years): 42.1

Estimated biological age (years): 23.8

Percentage of short telomeres (<3Kb): 13.08

Percentile of percentage of short telomeres: 14.99

Median telomere length (Kb): 6.929

Percentile of median telomere length: 55.75

IMPORTANT

In order to carry out any longitudinal analysis of
your telomere length and estimated biological
age, please record the code of this report for
future measurements.

CODE: USAZ003035RE

LIFE LENGTH

Results Summary—Patient Number 3 (MM)

Sex	Male
Chronological Age (in Years)	42.1
Estimated Biological Age (in Years)	23.8
Amount of Years in Program	9.0
Percentage of Short Telomeres (<3 Kb)	13.08
Percentile of Percentage of Short Telomeres	14.99
Median Telomere Length (Kb)	6.929
Percentile of Median Telomere Length	55.75

The percentages and percentiles that appear above are calculated from an extensive database of varied patients, enabling scientists and medical professionals to determine the ideal percentage of telomere length for specific chronological ages. By studying this data, individuals can learn about their biological age by determining where they fall in the chronological age spectrum. They can then develop an appropriate protocol for reversing biological age,[2] and they can then know whether that protocol works by doing a second measurement at a future point in time.

As the collective data in the tables above clearly illustrates, the percentage of short telomeres in a human's DNA has a direct impact on that individual's biological age. (Short telomeres, also referred to as critically short telomeres, are those less than 3 kilobases [Kb] in length, or with fewer than 3,000 base pairs. Initial telomere length can be approximately 10,000 to 15,000 base pairs, or less than 1/10,000 the length of the average chromosome. A base pair refers to the millions of pairs of nucleic acids [DNA].[3])

As individuals age, their percentage of short telomeres increases because of cellular replication. That is, every time a cell divides, telomere degradation (shortening) occurs. The length of time on the program recommended in this book helps to minimize this as much as possible, as we can see from the data of the individual who has been on the program for the longest amount of time (patient number 2): he is the oldest chronologically, but the median length of his telomeres is the closest to optimal, and his percentages are the most advantageous as well. To think of all this in layman's terms, people with a greater number of optimal-length telomeres will be biologically "younger"; thus, they will enjoy better health for a longer time, attaining the full life span without the attendant diseases and infirmities of so-called "old age."

Clearly, the ideal result is to have as many telomeres of optimal length as possible. This bears repeating in order to emphasize its critical importance: time and time again, among all patients and groups studied, the data illustrates that individuals with a greater amount of optimal-length telomeres live longer and enjoy lasting good health.

> Individuals with a greater amount of optimal-length telomeres live longer—and maintain good health throughout the life span.

The Program Defined

Again, the three individuals whose data appears above have been on the program for varying amounts of time, as specified. In all cases, "the program" refers to the total hormone supplementation/replacement therapy program (see the US Patent abstract in chapter 2). Basically, this means that each individual has received replenishment/supplementation of key hormones and nutrients at optimum levels during the entire time that he or she is on the program. (Optimum levels are those of a healthy 20-year-old male or female, depending upon the sex of each individual patient.)

The table below shows the hormones and nutrients that need to be at optimum levels.

Key Hormones

Human growth hormone (HGH)
Melatonin (pineal hormone)
T3 and T4 (thyroid hormones)

DHEA (dehydro-epiandosterone) (adrenal hormone)
Pregnenolone (adrenal hormone)
Cortisol (adrenal hormone)
Estrogen (female sex hormone)
Progesterone (female sex hormone)
Testosterone (male and female sex hormone)

Key Nutrients

Multiple vitamins and minerals
Multiple amino acids
Essential fatty acids (omega-3 and omega-6)
Vitamin D_3

[**NOTE:** *Cortisol (measured in the morning primarily, but then again more thoroughly 4 times in a 24-hour day), vitamin D, multiple vitamins and minerals, multiple amino acids, and essential fatty acids are not included in the US Patent abstract (see chapter 2). However, these all have been found to play crucial roles in attaining and maintaining good health and achieving the full life span. As a result, all are now used as part of the total hormone supplementation/replacement therapy program.*]

Remember from our discussion in chapter 2 that the enzyme telomerase maintains and repairs short telomeres, so the key to optimal-length telomeres is telomerase activation. Because telomerase is not yet available for supplementation use, medical practitioners must instead use hormone supplementation/ replacement therapy in order to activate telomerase.[4] In addition, the vitamins, minerals, and nutrients listed above all play an essential role in this process.

The total hormone supplementation/replacement therapy program seeks to achieve and maintain the ideal balance of hormones and nutrients in the human body, with the ultimate goal of lasting good health and longevity. The three patients whose data we studied in this chapter prove that the program works, as we can readily discern—and as patients in the program all undoubtedly affirm. And so now we will shift our attention to a deeper study of the program.

> Supplementation therapy seeks to achieve and maintain the ideal balance of hormones and nutrients in the human body.

[**NOTE:** *Throughout this book, descriptions of hormone replenishment/supplementation therapy and diet/nutrition supplementation refer to therapies and modalities administered by a medical professional and accompanied by appropriate monitoring on a regular basis. The information, ideas, and suggestions in this book are not intended as a substitute for professional medical advice or professional mental health advice. Before following any suggestions contained in this book, you should consult your personal physician and/or personal mental health professional.*]

Many people are already aware that stem cells rejuvenate the human body by replacing the cells that have died as a result of aging or injury. We will examine the connection between stem cells and hormones in the next chapter.

4

WHICH BIOIDENTICAL HORMONES ARE RELATED TO YOUR STEM CELLS IN REGENERATION AND REJUVENATION?

It was, of course, a grand and impressive thing to do, to mistrust the obvious, and to pin one's faith in things which could not be seen!

—Galen

Overview

As most people today know, stem cells play an essential role in tissue regeneration. They replace cells that have died as a result of the aging process. (Stem cells also are responsible for regeneration and rejuvenation following cellular injury or damage that is not related to the aging process.) Let's now turn our attention to the connection between hormones and stem cells.

> Stem cells are key to regeneration, rejuvenation, good health, well-being, and longevity.

[AUTHOR'S NOTE: *Throughout this book, HGH and GH are used interchangeably to refer to the (human) growth hormone.*]

What Are Stem Cells?

Stem Cells Defined

In simplest terms, a stem cell is an unspecified cell that can both self-renew (i.e., reproduce itself) and differentiate into many types of mature cells. (from collagen, to skin, to cartilage, to heart, to lung, to pancreas, and so on.) Consequently, stem cells are a key component of attaining and maintaining good health and well-being across the life span, and of achieving the full 120 years promised to us by God in Genesis 6:3. This is because stem cells have the capability to change into other types of cells, which gives them enormous regenerative and rejuvenating power. In other words, stem cells can keep us young and in prime health!

Most of the FDA-approved stem-cell therapy in the United States today is autologous. Autologous stem cells are stem cells taken from the same individual who will receive the graft of the extracted stem cells. (In other words, *autologous* means that the individual is both the donor and the recipient.)

The Basics of Stem-Cell Therapy

Stem cells can be collected from peripheral blood, adipose (fat) tissue or bone marrow. Adipose tissues have more stem cells but fewer growth factors, while peripheral blood cells have fewer stem cells but more growth factors in the plasma component of the blood. Therefore, a combination of these two sources of stem cells—peripheral blood cells and adipose tissue—offers the best of both worlds, so to speak, allowing for more stem cells and more growth factors. In addition, collection of stem cells from peripheral blood cells and adipose tissue is less painful than collection from bone marrow while yielding more stem cells than bone marrow.

It is widely known that the age of the donor and the donor's level of growth factors, such as IGF-1 (insulin growth factor), HGH (human growth hormone), testosterone, and estrogen, are directly proportional to the quantity and quality of the donor's stem cells.[1] (Remember, in the case of autologous stem-cell therapy, the same individual is both donor and recipient.) Thus, total hormone supplementation/replacement program plays an essential role in stem cells. In order to have a good quantity and quality of stem cells collected, we check the levels of growth factors in the donor before starting therapy (see essential hormones listed in the table below).

Essential Hormones in Stem-Cell Therapy

Insulin Growth Factors, Beta FGF 4, OCT4, SOX2, KLF4, C-MYC,
HGH
Testosterone (male and female sex hormone)
Estrogen (female sex hormone)
Pregnenolone
Thyroid Hormone
Melatonin Hormone

The above-listed hormones are essential to stem cells because their levels represent the quality and the quantity of a person's stem cells existing at that time.

IGF-1 is a growth-hormone-related protein and a growth factor used to measure and estimate the level of growth hormone (HGH) in the body. IGF-1 is used in this manner because the level of HGH in the body fluctuates from hour to hour during the course of every day (24-hour period), but the level of IGF-1 does not fluctuate.

Let's take a closer look at the ways in which hormones and stem cells work together to improve health and wellness, to effect cellular regeneration, to rejuvenate the body, and to make longevity with sustained well-being possible for everyone, fulfilling God's promised 120-year life span for each and every one of us.

> Because of their regenerative and rejuvenating power, stem cells can keep us young and in prime health!

The Role of Bio-identical Hormones and Growth Factors in Stem Cells

IGF-1, HGH, and other Growth Factors.

As we've already explained, IGF-1 is a growth-hormone-related protein and a growth factor that we use to measure and estimate the level of HGH in each individual. Again, we use IGF-1 for this purpose because the level of HGH in the body fluctuates on an hourly basis throughout every 24-hour period, whereas the level of IGF-1 in the body does not fluctuate. Let's more deeply examine the scientific findings related to IGF-1, HGH, and stem-cell growth.

Life Technologies in Maryland has conducted much research in this area. Their researchers have reported the increase of cell growth in studies of human stem cells cultured in IGF-1(4 µg/ml) of controlled medium. This growth was reported after six days in the culture, at which time cell numbers increased from 100,000 to 500,000.[2]

Researchers at the University of Wurzburg in Germany have reached similar conclusions and have in fact expanded upon the results described above. To summarize the conclusions of my German colleagues, "Age-dependent impairment of stem cells is corrected by growth hormone-mediated increase of IGF-1."[3]

The Wurzburg research team further reported the following results from studies of middle-aged (57.4, plus or minus 1.4 years) males, as well as elderly (older than 58.8) and young (younger than 56) male subjects:[4]

- Growth hormone treatment in middle-aged subjects elevated IGF-1 levels and increased circulating stem cells, with improved colony forming and migratory capacity comparable to that of the younger subjects.
- IGF-1 stimulated stem-cell differentiation, migratory capacity, and the ability to incorporate into forming vascular networks in vitro via the IGF-1 receptor.
- IGF-1 increased telomerase activity.
- Growth-hormone-mediated increase in IGF-1 reverses age-related stem-cell dysfunction.
- IGF-1 improved function and attenuated cellular senescence (reduced cell vitality caused by aging) in elderly subjects.

Furthermore, cellular aging is associated with an increased risk for atherosclerosis (so-called hardening of the arteries), a possible cause of which is low stem-cell numbers and dysfunctional endothelial stem cells that insufficiently repair damaged vascular walls. (Endothelial cells line the interior surface of blood vessels and lymphatic vessels.) Growth-hormone-mediated increase of IGF-1 improved the situation in the subjects in the Wurzburg study who received growth hormone (recombinant GH 0.4 mg/d) over a ten-day period.[5]

Conducting separate studies related to the administration of growth hormone, medical researchers in Texas have reported conclusions similar to what we have discussed thus far. Specifically, GH administration selectively augments the outgrowth of stem-cell population in healthy individuals, which supports GH replacement in the setting of adult GH deficiency in order to maintain vascular integrity; "this has positive implications for the use of GH in future regenerative cell-based therapies."[6]

Furthermore, the decrease in stem cells observed as part of the aging process may in part be explained by the decline of GH, thereby contributing to cardiovascular senescence (aging/ deterioration).[7] The Texas research team's studies suggest that stem cells impact vascular health by modulating vascular repair and function: current evidence demonstrates that both the number of stem cells and their functionality are restored/ regenerated as a result of growth-hormone-mediated IGF-1; therefore, modulation of GH and IGF-1 may provide a useful therapy in the prevention of age-associated changes in the cardiovascular system and in future regenerative cell-based therapies.[8]

The supportive findings continue. Another research team in the Netherlands, working independently of the teams described above, concluded that one year of recombinant GH replacement in adults with GH deficiency improved endothelial function and increased the number of circulating stem cells,[9] which strengthens and corroborates the conclusions discussed thus far.

In 2012, the Nobel Prize in Medicine was awarded to Dr. Yamanaka who, continuing the work of British scientist Dr. Gurdon, discovered that reprogramming in cells (for example an adipose tissue cell) can be accomplished by just four transcription factors (OCT4, SOX2, KLF4, C-MYC.) Transcription factors are proteins made by master genes to regulate other genes. By injecting the four transcription factors into an adult cell of any type, Dr. Yamanaka showed that he could lead the cell back to its primitive, or stem cell, form.

This type of discovery shows how important it is to have these growth factors, which are in the plasma of the donor, be transplanted together and at the same time with the adipose tissue cells in cosmetic procedures.

Now that we have thoroughly examined the importance of IGF-1, HGH and Growth Factors, let's explore some of the other essential hormones as related to the quantity and quality of the stem cells in our bodies, and to the total hormone supplementation/replacement therapy program.

Estrogen and Pregnenolone Influence the Quantity and Quality of the Stem Cells in Our Bodies

Let's examine the effects of estrogen on stem cells and the human body's capacity for cellular regeneration/rejuvenation. (Remember that estrogen is a female sex hormone.) In general, estrogen offers significant benefits among diverse stem-cell populations. Specifically, estrogen increases the proliferation of embryonic neural stem cells and accelerates differentiation of neurons during neurogenesis (growth of nerve cells), which suggests that estrogen may play a role in transplantation of neural stem cells as part of a therapeutic approach to neurodegenerative disease.[10] Separate clinical research on estrogen indicates that premenopausal women presented the highest level of circulating stem cells (1.4 per 10,000 cells), while postmenopausal women presented the lowest (4 per 1,000,000 cells); moreover, the level of stem cells increased significantly with bio-identical hormone replacement therapy, on average by 25.5 percent.[11]

Another key hormone, pregnenolone, promotes the proliferation of human stem cells (also called *progenitor cells*)[12], making pregnenolone vital to both stem-cell therapy and the total hormone replacement/supplementation therapy program.

Thyroid Hormones and Melatonin Hormone Also Influence the Quantity and Quality of Our Stem Cells

Whereas pregnenolone works to proliferate stem cells in a more aggregate manner, T3 (a thyroid hormone) promotes cardiac differentiation and maturation of embryonic stem cells; that is, embryonic stem cells can differentiate into functional cardiomyocytes (cardiac-muscle cells), meaning that T3 promotes stem-cell growth of heart-muscle tissue.[13]

Finally, we must consider melatonin, which behaves as a preconditioning agent that increases the survival of stem cells. Using melatonin for pretreatment of stem cells may represent a new and safer approach to improving the beneficial effects of stem-cell therapy administered to solid organs, as appeared to be the case following an intraparenchymal injection of melatonin into an ischemic kidney.[14] (The kidney was considered ischemic because of a deficient supply of blood as a result of an obstructed inflow of arterial blood to the organ.)

With each passing day, more innovative and exciting research takes place in the groundbreaking field of stem-cell therapy. To be sure, the findings will only proliferate, reinforcing our existing knowledge that bio-identical hormones all play an essential role in maintaining the quantity and quality of the stem cells in our bodies.

> Stem-cell growth is a key component of any regenerative cell-based therapy, and it is also key to living longer and in better health.

In the next chapter, we will explain and describe in greater detail the medical technology/modality employed in our recommended method of hormone supplementation/replacement therapy and vitamin/nutrient supplementation.

5

THE METHOD AND MEDICAL TECHNOLOGY OF THE 21ST CENTURY— HOW TO REVERSE BIOLOGICAL AGE, ATTAIN BETTER HEALTH, AND INCREASE THE LIFE SPAN[1]

The doctor of the future will give no medicine, but will interest her or his patients in the care of the human frame, in a proper diet, and in the cause and prevention of disease.

—Thomas Alva Edison

Overview

We have been discussing the modality of the total hormone supplementation/replacement therapy program throughout the previous chapters of this book. Now we will turn our attention to a deeper exploration of that modality. This chapter will provide the actual method and medical technology recommended for reversing biological age, attaining better health, and increasing the life span.

Much of the recommended method and medical technology is rather scientific and technical, but it is necessary to understand the terminology and its application in order to have a clear picture of the program and all that it offers patients. Let's strive to understand as much of the science as possible so that we will be well informed about longevity and good health; then, and only then, can we make optimal decisions about what we need to do in order to ensure our own enduring well-being.

> Balanced hormones and nutrients are key to the recommended method for reversing biological age, attaining better health, and increasing the life span.

Reversing Biological Age, Attaining Better Health, and Increasing the Life Span

The Method Defined and Described

To briefly summarize what we've already discussed, particularly in chapters 2 and 3, the medical technology patented in the total hormone supplementation/replacement therapy program in 1999 (see US Patent abstract in chapter 2) was discovered in the early 1990s, following decades of research and study of the relationship between bio-identical hormones and telomerase,[2] as enumerated throughout the previous sections of this book.

As we have seen throughout our discussion, telomeres and telomerase are essential to reversing biological age and thereby increasing longevity—by which we do not mean merely living more years, but rather attaining the full life span with attendant good health and vitality. When the majority of telomeres in their DNA are of optimal length, individuals can live longer and in better health.

The total hormone supplementation/replacement therapy program offers the potential to achieve all this. It might sound like magic—or a miracle—but in actuality it is cellular science. Technically, this science *is* a miracle: God's promised 120-year life span (see chapter 1). We will further explore the "miracle" component when we discuss our individual responsibility for our health and well-being, as well as the body-mind-spirit connection and the dynamic it creates for our total wellness. For now, let's focus on the science that makes the method and medical technology possible.

To review the simplest aspects first, part of the program is the same as any healthful regimen: proper diet and nutrition, regular exercise,* and a strong body-mind-spirit connection and overall wellness dynamic. Now for the more complicated aspects—or at least the scientific and technical ones.

Checking and Assessing Hormone Levels

The key to the program is maintaining optimal hormone levels at all times. In essence, good health is about balance. To use scientific terminology, this is *homeostasis,* when every system in the body is functioning optimally. Homeostasis—or perfect balance within all body systems—means total good health and well-being across the life span, even to 120 . . . and beyond.

---

* The information, ideas, and suggestions in this book are not intended as a substitute for professional medical advice or professional mental health advice. Before following any suggestions contained in this book, you should consult your personal physician and/or personal mental health professional. Neither the author nor the publisher shall be liable or responsible for any loss or damage allegedly arising as a consequence of your use or application of any information or suggestions in this book.

Furthermore, by maintaining optimal hormone levels (which means the levels of a healthy 20-year-old), we can cure many age-related diseases and infirmities[3] and even reverse our biological age. (Remember, as described in the preface, I am chronologically 61, but biologically I am only 33.9!)

The hormones we need to keep in balance are the same ones we discussed in the previous chapter, but let's list them here again.

Key Hormones

Human growth hormone (HGH)
Melatonin (pineal hormone)
T3 and T4 (thyroid hormones)
DHEA (dehydro-epiandosterone) (adrenal hormone)
Pregnenolone (adrenal hormone)
Cortisol (adrenal hormone)
Estrogen (female sex hormone)
Progesterone (female sex hormone)
Testosterone (male and female sex hormone)

We can assess these hormone levels by means of simple blood analysis; the optimal ranges of a healthy 20-year-old are provided on the analyses prepared by almost every medical laboratory. With the requisite data determined, all that is necessary is a qualified physician who can optimize the hormone levels as needed.

A word of caution: only *bio-identical hormones* can be used in supplementation[4]; that is, hormones that have the same structure as the ones God gave every human. Synthetic hormones—hormones that are in any way different from our natural ones, no matter how seemingly insignificant such differences might be—can cause negative side effects and even cancer. God gave us the intelligence and talent to discover how to achieve the life span he promised, but he would never want us to put anything into our bodies that he had not put there or that he did not create for us. As mentioned previously, this book is not intended as a spiritual exegesis; however, part of attaining and maintaining good health and a full life span is understanding that God wants us to live long and be healthy—but to do so naturally, not synthetically.

Now let's turn our attention to how to do exactly that: live longer and healthier . . . naturally.

> Only bio-identical hormones can be used in supplementation because natural, not synthetic, methods are what will help us achieve the optimal balance needed for total wellness and longevity.

Tests Needed for Telomerase Activation Therapy—Women

IGF-1 and IGF Binding Protein-3 (insulin growth factor)
Free T3 (*not* T3 uptake), Free T4, TSH (thyroid stimulating hormone) (thyroid hormones)
DHEA (dehydro-epiandosterone) *or* **DHEA Sulfate** (adrenal hormones)
Morning Cortisol or 4 Measurements throughout 24 hours (adrenal hormone)
Pregnenolone (adrenal hormone made for the maintenance of nerves and brain)
Total Testosterone *and* **Free Testosterone** (male and female sex hormone)

Estradiol (E2) (estrogen)   (female sex hormone)
Progesterone   (female sex hormone; test best taken on day 20 to 23 of cycle   for premenopausal women)
FSH (follicle stimulating hormone)   (female sex hormone)
Fasting Insulin   (peptide hormone)
CRP (C-Reactive Protein or Cold-Reactive Protein)   (blood protein)
Serum Vitamin D Level
Chemistry 24   (blood panel including the three tests below)
- **Fasting Glucose**
- **Lipids**
- **Liver Enzymes**
CBC (complete blood count) with Differential
Complete Urinalysis with Microscopic Examination and Counts of Cells   (morning awaking urine specimen)
8-Hour Collection of Urine for Environmental Chemical Toxins
Toxic Heavy Metals Screening Hair Test (by Genova)
Morning Awaking Oral Temperature by Mercury-like Thermometer or Welch-Allyn Digital Thermometer (*not* other digital thermometers)
Afternoon (between 1 and 4 p.m.) Oral Temperature by Mercury-like Thermometer or Welch-Allyn Digital Thermometer (*not* other digital thermometers)

H-Scan ("Age Scan")
(a performance test of biological age, determined by functions of various body systems, such as auditory and visual reaction times, pulmonary functions, speed of motor functions, memory, etc.)
<u>OPTIONAL</u>:
Telomere Length Test
(test of biological age, determined by length of telomeres in the DNA [by Life Length Inc.])

[**NOTE:** *Total cost for the above-captioned tests should not exceed US $590 in 2013.*]

Tests Needed for Telomerase Activation Therapy—Men

IGF-1 and IGF Binding Protein-3 (insulin growth factor)
Free T3 (*not* T3 uptake), **Free T4, TSH** (thyroid stimulating hormone) (thyroid hormones)
DHEA (dehydro-epiandosterone) <u>OR</u> **DHEA Sulfate** (adrenal hormones)
Morning Cortisol or 4 Measurements throughout 24 hours (adrenal hormone)
Pregnenolone (adrenal hormone made for the maintenance of nerves and brain)
Total Testosterone *and* **Free Testosterone** (male and female sex hormone)
PSA (prostate-specific antigen) (glycoprotein enzyme)
Fasting Insulin (peptide hormone)

CRP (C-Reactive Protein or Cold-Reactive Protein) (blood protein)
Serum Vitamin D Level
Chemistry 24 (blood panel including the three tests below)
- **Fasting Glucose**
- **Lipids**
- **Liver Enzymes**
CBC (complete blood count) with Differential
Complete Urinalysis with Microscopic Examination and Counts of Cells (morning awaking urine specimen)
8-Hour Collection of Urine for Environmental Chemical Toxins
Toxic Heavy Metals Screening Hair Test (by Genova)
Morning Awaking Oral Temperature by Mercury-like Thermometer or Welch-Allyn Digital Thermometer (*not* other digital thermometers)
Afternoon (between 1 and 4 p.m.) Oral Temperature by Mercury-like Thermometer or Welch-Allyn Digital Thermometer (*not* other digital thermometers)
H-Scan ("Age Scan") (a performance test of biological age, determined by functions of various body systems, such as auditory and visual reaction times, pulmonary functions, speed of motor functions, memory, etc.)
<u>**OPTIONAL**</u>:
Telomere Length Test (test of biological age, determined by length of telomeres in the DNA [by Life Length Inc.])

[**NOTE:** *Total cost for the above-captioned tests should not exceed US $590 in 2013.*]

The tests used in the actual total hormone supplementation/ replacement therapy program are more extensive than those listed in previous chapters and in the US Patent (see chapter 2). Continual work with patients has led to several critical discoveries, including, but not limited to, the importance of monitoring

- cortisol levels,
- fasting insulin levels,
- serum vitamin D levels, and
- chemistry 24 blood panel.

Let's consider the added tests listed above in deeper detail.

Monitoring cortisol and supplementing it when it is deficient (based on blood-test analyses) is efficacious for anti-aging protocols.

Monitoring fasting insulin levels checks for diabetes, prediabetes, and pancreatic health.

Similarly, the Chemistry 24 blood panel, which monitors glucose, lipids, and liver enzymes, assesses the health of the kidneys, liver, and pancreas. The health of these three organs is essential to overall wellness and longevity.

Vitamin D plays a key hormonal role in preventing cancer, heart disease, and many other age-related diseases; the FDA-recommended minimum requirement (which is what most multivitamins contain) is not adequate for achieving the level necessary for the longevity goals recommended here. Essential fatty acids, which we must obtain from our diet because the human body cannot produce them, play important roles in controlling cholesterol, inflammation, and DNA transcriptions.[5]

Thus, all the tests listed in this chapter are extremely important for patients to have, as the results are key to developing a comprehensive protocol for total wellness. Once all the hormone levels are optimal (the same as those of a healthy 20-year-old), the body will be in balance, and then the individual can attain and maintain good health ongoing—and, ultimately, achieve the full life span with attendant vitality and total well-being.

Now that we understand the importance of optimal hormone levels, we must further examine the interrelationship of hormones, telomeres, and telomerase that we began to explore in previous chapters.

[**NOTE:** *Throughout this book, descriptions of hormone replenishment/supplementation therapy and diet/nutrition supplementation refer to therapies and modalities administered by a medical professional, and accompanied by appropriate monitoring on a regular basis. The information, ideas, and suggestions in this book are not intended as a substitute for professional medical advice or professional mental health advice. Before following any suggestions contained in this book, you should consult your personal physician and/or personal mental health professional.*]

> Optimal hormone levels lead to good health throughout the life span: living longer and with increased vitality.

Why Telomeres Are Important

We have already discussed the importance of telomeres and telomerase as part of the anti-aging/longevity process, but, as we consider the efficacy of the total hormone supplementation/ replacement therapy program, let's just take a moment to reemphasize the critical roles telomeres and telomerase play in attaining and maintaining overall wellness and long life.

Telomeres are important because they protect and preserve our chromosomes, thereby preventing—or, at least, limiting—DNA degradation. Consequently, telomeres are essential to the optimal functionality, viability, and vitality of our cells. Although telomere shortening occurs naturally as part of cell division, in order to achieve longevity in continued good health, humans must ideally have as many optimal-length telomeres as possible.[6]

Telomerase is the enzyme that maintains and repairs telomeres, elongating short telomeres to their optimal length.[7] Remember, this optimal length can reverse biological age, minimizing and even eliminating the diseases and infirmities of so-called "old age." Control of telomere length also has the potential to treat many diseases associated with aging, as we have seen, thereby allowing humans to attain the God-promised age of 120, and to do so with sustained good health and well-being, vibrant and vital throughout the life span.

> Telomeres are essential to the optimal functionality, viability, and vitality of every cell in the human body.

Telomere Length and Its Significance

Again, telomeres shorten as part of cell division. This is a natural process, but it leads to the cellular degradation and the journey to death that we call aging. Simply stated, it is ideal to have as many optimal-length telomeres as possible. The more telomeres of optimal length that a person has, the greater chance he or she has to reverse biological age, as indicated by the data of the patients observed in chapter 3 and my own data in the preface.

As we've seen, medical practitioners can monitor the percentage of short telomere length in order to achieve a greater number of optimal-length telomeres. The recommended total hormone supplementation/replacement therapy is the most efficacious method to use at this moment in time. This method and medical technology lead to the desired balance of hormones and nutrients that the human body needs in order to reverse biological age, improve overall health, and attain the full life span in a state of enduring wellness, vitality, and vibrancy.

So, in essence, telomere length is the most significant contributor to lasting good health and longevity. The big picture of overall health, wellness, and longevity hinges on a tiny, microscopic cellular structure: the telomere.

> The big picture of overall health, wellness, and longevity hinges on the tiny telomere.

Telomere Length's Impact on Biological Age

Remember that biological age is an excellent indicator of any individual's overall health. It goes without saying that anyone whose biological age is less than his or her chronological age must be in excellent health, as the patients observed in chapter 3 illustrate. Again using myself as an example, my chronological age is 61, but my biological age is only 33.9. Telomere length is crucial to that difference. Individuals with a lot of short telomeres will not have biological ages of almost half that of their chronological age: it is not scientifically possible.

For all these reasons, it is critical for individuals to determine the percentage of short telomeres in their cells. Once in possession of the data from their own cells, as tested, they can seek out skilled physicians who will customize a program for them, designed to regain the optimal balance of hormones and nutrients that will repair and lengthen short telomeres, resulting in better health and longer life. The recommended method of total hormone supplementation/replacement therapy keeps that ultimate goal at the forefront of the program at all times and for every patient. (Individuals should repeat the telomere measurement [a blood test] once a year.)

> Individuals with a lot of short telomeres will not succeed in reversing biological age.

Understanding Biological Age versus Chronological Age

The difference between biological and chronological age is probably the simplest concept defined in this book: *biological age* refers to the health of our cells; *chronological age* refers to the years we have attained. Again, as described, my biological age is 33.9, while my chronological age is 61. This means that my cells are as healthy as those of an average 33-year-old.

We all love to hear people say, "You look so young! I never would have guessed your age!" Such statements refer to chronological age, of course. Even better than not looking our age is not feeling our age. By reversing biological age, we can look and feel years younger than the calendar tells us we are. Rest assured that this feels as wonderful as it sounds! It truly is the manifestation of God's promised 120-year life span, with the wellness and vitality he most assuredly intended to accompany us throughout all the years of a full life.

In simplest terms, then, biological and chronological age are easy to understand.

However, the importance of biological age goes far beyond the benefits of looking and feeling younger than the number indicated by our date of birth. Biological age provides a window into human health. Knowing our biological age allows us to obtain a better understanding of how lifestyle choices, behaviors, habits, and the environment all impact aging. Once we know our own data, so to speak, we have the opportunity to make appropriate changes—that is, the ones necessary to cultivate and maintain good health and to attain the full life span. Then, after making those necessary changes, we can periodically retest our DNA, measuring the results with the assistance of a trained physician.

Thus, we can see that it is absolutely essential to determine and monitor our biological age, and telomere testing is the most efficacious method for that determination and monitoring.

> Biological age provides a window into human health.

Telomere Analysis

Telomere analysis refers to the full system of measuring each individual's telomeres and calculating the percentage of short telomeres. That analysis allows medical professionals to recommend an appropriate protocol for anti-aging, total health, and longevity (such as the total hormone supplementation/ replacement therapy program).

As we've seen, telomere length provides information about the individual's biological age, which enables medical professionals to develop a good picture of his or her overall health and wellness. Armed with that information, physicians can then custom craft a plan/protocol for that person, designed to achieve body balance and lasting health throughout the life span.

Accordingly, let's review the component tests of telomere analysis.

> Telomere analysis is one part of a total health, wellness, and longevity plan.

Test Procedures and Protocols: TAT, HT Q-FISH, PCR

Several test procedures and protocols exist, but those provided by the Life Length Institute[8] are optimal. We will describe Life Length's Telomere Analysis Technology (TAT) and High Throughput Quantitative Fluorescent in Situ Hybridization (HT Q-FISH) first, and then explain another available test (polymerase chain reaction [PCR]), in order to provide a full overview of the options.

[**NOTE:** *The full scientific/technical details of these tests are beyond the scope of this book; descriptions here are provided for basic overview purposes only. For a deeper description, please visit www.lifelength.com.*]

TAT

Life Length's Telomere Analysis Technology (TAT) comprises two established protocols that allow the determination of telomere length at the individual level, both from cellular samples (HT Q-FISH [see below]) and tissue samples (Telomapping). HT Q-FISH technique is primarily used to measure telomere length on blood-cell samples, but it can be used on any type of cellular sample.[9] (HT Q-FISH is the more commonly utilized technique, so our discussion will not examine Telomapping.)

HT Q-FISH

In the High Throughput Quantitative Fluorescent in Situ Hybridization (HT Q-FISH) technique, telomeres are hybridized by means of a telomeric probe labeled with fluorescence. Each probe recognizes a fixed number of telomeric repeats (base pairs). As a result, the intensity of the fluorescent signal from the probes that hybridize to a given telomere is directly proportional to telomere length. Finally, the fluorescence values are transformed into telomere-length values for each individual telomere spot within a cell, which enables measurement of the mean telomere length, as well as the percentage of short telomeres in a cell population.[10]

Although, as stated, the full scientific implications of the HT Q-FISH are beyond the scope of this book, understanding this test's use is crucial to our discussion. The most important thing to know about the HT Q-FISH is that it basically measures the telomeres in cell nuclei taken from blood samples. As we've seen, telomere length provides information about the individual's biological age, which enables medical professionals to develop a good picture of the patient's overall health and wellness. Based on that data and information, such physicians can then custom craft a plan/protocol for each person, designed to achieve body balance and lasting health throughout the life span.

PCR

Polymerase chain reaction (PCR) is another high throughput telomere-length measurement test (as are flow cyclometry methods), but these procedures can only determine the mean telomere length of cell or sample; they are unable to measure the actual cause of aging and its effects, which is the percentage of short telomeres. Slight changes in the percentages of short telomeres that occur with aging, lifestyle, and/or quality of life are not reflected in mean telomere length.[11]

Why TAT Is Optimal

The above explanation of PCR shows why Life Length's TAT is the optimal system for telomere analysis. TAT is extremely accurate and so sensitive that it can measure telomeres down to 120 base pairs. (In layman's terms, that would be equivalent to measuring a 150,000-kilometer highway and being precise within 120 meters.) Remember too that critically short telomeres are those that have shortened to fewer than 3,000 base pairs; initial telomere length can be approximately 10,000 to 15,000 base pairs, or less than 1/10,000 the length of the average chromosome.[12]

Using Life Length's TAT and HT Q-FISH, telomere length can be measured with as little as 300 microliters of blood, but the typical—and optimal—blood draw is 6 milliliters, in order to achieve the best replicability and maintain proper sample control.

> TAT is the optimal system for obtaining accurate telomere analysis.

Follow-up

Following the initial TAT procedures, patients should be tested annually in order to monitor telomere length and short-telomere percentages. Patients with a large percentage of critically short telomeres should repeat the tests every six months or every three months, depending upon their physicians' recommendations.* Regular, accurate monitoring of

---

* Throughout this book, descriptions of hormone replenishment/ supplementation therapy and diet/nutrition supplementation refer to therapies and modalities administered by a medical professional, and accompanied by appropriate monitoring on a regular basis. The

telomere length enables physicians to alter patients' individual customized plans/protocols as needed, based on any changes in telomere length and/or percentages detected in the tests. As previously described, this customization of the total hormone supplementation/replacement therapy plan is crucial to design, as its intention is to allow the individual to achieve body balance and lasting health throughout the life span.

> Individual customization of the total hormone supplementation/replacement therapy plan is designed to achieve body balance and lasting health throughout the life span.

Having extensively explained and described the method and medical technology of the total hormone supplementation/ replacement therapy plan, we can now turn our attention to the difference between hormone supplementation and nutrition. That will be the topic of the next chapter, in which we will explain and describe the proper ways to achieve body balance.

[**AUTHOR'S NOTE:** *If you are interested in the recommended protocol(s) described throughout this chapter but are unable to obtain a prescription for these tests from your own physician, you can obtain a complimentary prescription (doctor's order) by e-mailing me at edmundchein@yahoo.com or check.your. hormones@gmail.com.*]

---

information, ideas, and suggestions in this book are not intended as a substitute for professional medical advice or professional mental health advice. Before following any suggestions contained in this book, you should consult your personal physician and/or personal mental health professional.

6

THE DELICATE BALANCE OF A STRONG BODY—THE DIFFERENCE BETWEEN HORMONE SUPPLEMENTATION AND NUTRITION/EXERCISE

Healing is making whole, restoring a state of perfection and balance that has been lost through illness or injury.

—Andrew Weil, MD

Overview

Now that we have extensively explored the method and medical technology of the total hormone supplementation/replacement therapy program, it is time to focus on the ways to achieve optimal balance within all systems of the body. Accordingly, we will examine all the components of total system balance necessary for enduring strength and resilience, which counteract aging, resulting in longevity with continued good health. Telomere length, hormone supplementation, nutrition, and exercise all play key roles in attaining—and maintaining—strength, resilience, and total wellness.

The goal of this chapter is to show what it means to truly be strong and healthy at every age and how maintaining that strength and good health will, in turn, ensure a long life. We will illustrate the differences between hormone supplementation and nutrition, explaining how to effectively use them, individually and together, in order to achieve optimal results. Supplementation programs should always be envisioned as enhancements to proper diet and regular exercise, which are essential to every effective health regimen.

[**NOTE:** *Throughout this book, descriptions of hormone replenishment/supplementation therapy and diet/nutrition supplementation refer to therapies and modalities administered by a medical professional, and accompanied by appropriate monitoring on a regular basis. The information, ideas, and suggestions in this book are not intended as a substitute for professional medical advice or professional mental health advice. Before following any suggestions contained in this book, you should consult your personal physician and/or personal mental health professional.*]

> Hormone supplementation and proper nutrition enable the achievement of optimal body balance, lasting good health, and long life.

Telomere Length and Good Health

We already know how essential telomere length is to good health. Optimal-length telomeres allow for the reversal of our biological age, which in turn increases longevity. To put this another way, reversing biological age—feeling and looking younger than the calendar reflects—means not just living longer, but doing so in consistent good health. Attaining the full life span with attendant good health and vitality is the essence of antiaging and longevity. Telomeres hold the key to achieving all this.

To briefly review how and why all this is the case, remember that telomeres shorten as part of cell division. Although this is a natural process, it leads to cellular degradation. We call that degradation (also known as "cell death") aging. This makes it easy to see why it is ideal to have as many optimal-length telomeres as possible: the more telomeres of optimal length that a person has, the greater chance he or she has to reverse biological age. (The data of the patients observed in chapter 3 provide quantifiable illustration of this.)

> When the majority of telomeres in their DNA are of optimal length, individuals can live longer and in better health.

Hormones and Telomere Length

In chapter 5, we explained the method and medical technology for measuring telomere length. Using the data gleaned from the tests described, medical practitioners can then create customized plans designed to allow each patient to achieve a greater number of optimal-length telomeres. As stated—and as the data in previous chapters has shown—the recommended total hormone supplementation/replacement therapy is the most efficacious method to use. In essence, this method and medical technology lead to the desired balance of hormones and nutrients that the human body needs in order to reverse biological age, improve overall health, and attain the full life span in a state of enduring wellness, vitality, and vibrancy.

Remember, though, it all revolves around telomere length, which is the most significant contributor to lasting good health and longevity. It's a wonder that so much depends on a microscopic cellular structure, but it does. Without a majority of optimal-length telomeres, individuals cannot attain or maintain good health or long life.

We can consider the telomere as the portion of human DNA that controls the life span at the cellular level. Optimal-length telomeres have the potential to achieve "cellular immortality." To simplify the details of the scientific process, increasing the hormone level (using bio-identical hormone supplementation/ replacement therapy) signals the DNA of the mother (older) cells to work again. Once the DNA receives the signal that the body is that of a healthy 20-year-old, that DNA will accordingly reproduce healthy, biologically young daughter cells. In a nutshell, this is the process of reversing biological age.[1]

Why, then, are we unable to automatically reverse biological age? This question has no simple answer. Theoretically, and strictly following science, we *are* able to—or at least we have the potential to do so. The human body is designed to maintain and repair its telomeres. The enzyme telomerase serves this function, but, as we've seen, the aging process hinders its activation. However, certain hormones activate telomerase. This is why the recommended total hormone supplementation/replacement therapy program is so effective. The bio-identical hormones used in the program instruct the telomerase to repair shortened telomeres, allowing the body to maintain as many telomeres of optimal length as possible. Individuals on the program reverse biological age, improve total wellness, and live longer and in better health (see chapter 3).

> The total hormone supplementation/replacement therapy program enables individuals to reverse biological age, improve total wellness, and live longer and in better health.

Nutrients and Telomere Length

Hormone supplementation is an important component of any protocol designed to lengthen short telomeres. However, nutrients play a crucial role too. This means proper nutrition through a healthy diet, as well as nutrient supplementation.*

[NOTE: *Although a comprehensive diet recommendation is beyond the scope and intention of this book, a healthy diet mainly consists of eating plenty of fruits and vegetables, whole grains, moderate amounts of lean protein, and small amounts of polyunsaturated fats. The following items should be avoided: trans fats, monounsaturated fats, high-fructose corn syrup, preservatives, and artificial sweeteners, flavoring, and coloring. Individuals should consult their physicians to obtain appropriate specific dietary regimens, including appropriate intake of fiber, fluids, sugars, and sodium, as various conditions mandate different amounts of these.*]

Through extensive research and clinical studies, scientists have demonstrated that many nutrients are able to elongate telomeres. Such nutrients do not have as much power to elongate telomeres as hormones do. The difference between them is *potency.* Hormones are simply able to lengthen telomeres more quickly than nutrients are able to. In order to achieve the same result using nutrients alone, individuals will have to commit to long-term daily use. Thus, the optimal choice is the total hormone

---

* Throughout this book, descriptions of hormone replenishment/ supplementation therapy and diet/nutrition supplementation refer to therapies and modalities administered by a medical professional, and accompanied by appropriate monitoring on a regular basis. The information, ideas, and suggestions in this book are not intended as a substitute for professional medical advice or professional mental health advice. Before following any suggestions contained in this book, you should consult your personal physician and/or personal mental health professional.

supplementation/replacement therapy program, which utilizes a combination of key hormones and nutrients.

To review from chapter 3, the key hormones recommended are listed below. (The full program appears in chapter 5.)

Key Hormones

Human growth hormone (HGH)
Melatonin (pineal hormone)
T3 and T4 (thyroid hormones)
DHEA (dehydro-epiandosterone) (adrenal hormone)
Pregnenolone (adrenal hormone)
Cortisol (adrenal hormone)
Estrogen (female sex hormone)
Progesterone (female sex hormone)
Testosterone (male and female sex hormone)

Expanding on the nutrients described in chapter 3, the nutrients needed to lengthen telomeres appear in the table below.

Key Nutrients

Multiple vitamins and minerals
Multiple amino acids
Essential fatty acids (omega-3 and omega-6)
Vitamin D$_3$

To further describe the scientific studies mentioned above, Drs. Cattaneo, Farzaneh-Far, Furumoto, Kang, Nemoto, Richards, Tanaka, Xu, and Yokoo each conducted separate research on the following substances' positive effect on telomere lengthening: vitamin B$_{12}$ and folate[2]; omega-3 fatty acid[3]; vitamins C and E[4]; nicotinamide (vitamin B$_3$)[5]; zinc[6]; vitamin D[7]; and magnesium[8].

(Note that, as of this writing, the potency of these substances has not been compared.)

To review our discussion of nutrients in chapter 5, remember that vitamin D plays a key role in preventing cancer, heart disease, and many other age-related diseases; however, the FDA-recommended minimum requirement (which is what most multivitamins contain) is not adequate for achieving the level necessary for the longevity goals recommended here. Essential fatty acids, which we must obtain from our diet because the human body cannot produce them, play important roles in controlling cholesterol, inflammation, and DNA transcriptions.[9]

Now let's see how to use hormone supplementation/replacement in conjunction with, and as an enhancement to, a healthy regimen of proper diet and regular exercise.[*]

Addition, Not Subtraction—Hormone Supplementation Used to Enhance Diet and Exercise Plans

To reiterate, hormone supplementation is an enhancement of a healthy regimen of proper diet and regular exercise. Even when supplementation is used to replenish depleted hormone levels, it is always done in addition to diet and exercise, not as

---

[*] Throughout this book, descriptions of hormone replenishment/ supplementation therapy and diet/nutrition supplementation refer to therapies and modalities administered by a medical professional, and accompanied by appropriate monitoring on a regular basis. The information, ideas, and suggestions in this book are not intended as a substitute for professional medical advice or professional mental health advice. Before following any suggestions contained in this book, you should consult your personal physician and/or personal mental health professional.

a substitution for them. In other words, we don't ever subtract healthy diet and exercise, we simply add to them.

Fitness, Diet, and Exercise Gurus Who Died before the Age of 100

While the total hormone supplementation/replacement therapy program helps patients attain the full life span of 120 with attendant good health and well-being, <u>ALL of those</u> so-called fitness gurus did not even attain the age of 100. Most did not even reach the age of 80, and some died in their 50s and 60s. Let's look at several of these well-known and charismatic figures, examining the difference between the programs they espoused and promoted and the program described throughout this book.

Consider the famous fitness guru Jack LaLanne—the longest living of all the gurus. <u>No one could exercise more or eat more healthfully on a daily basis than he did</u>. And yet, he died in 2011 at the age of 96, following a bout with a simple case of influenza that led to pneumonia (reported cause of death).[10] His death indicated that his immune system (white blood cells and lymphocytes, etc.) could not, and did not, effectively fight off the infection. He had 24 years to go to attain the full life span, but he didn't. This means that his decades-long seeming fitness was insufficient to reverse his biological age, maintain true overall good health and wellness, and attain the God-promised age of 120.

Many other famous proponents of fitness, diet, and exercise had even shorter life spans than LaLanne's, which would indicate that their programs lacked the essential scientific components of longevity: balanced hormones and nutrients. (The total hormone supplementation/replacement therapy program, as described throughout this book, offers the medical technology and methodology necessary to achieve this ideal balance.)

Dr. Robert Atkins, creator of the famous Atkins Diet, basically gave the okay to eat a diet based on fat and protein, with carbohydrates (other than a limited amount of certain fruits and vegetables) severely restricted. In essence, Atkins condemned carbohydrates to the "hall of dietary shame." After his death in 2003 at the age of 72, it was revealed that Atkins himself had a history of serious heart problems, including myocardial infarction (heart attack), congestive heart failure, and hypertension. Some have suggested that these conditions led to his death, which was immediately caused by a fall on the ice. Others have maintained that his heart attack was caused by a chronic infection (low immunity).[11] (Robert Atkins's life span was 48 years shorter than the God-promised 120 years, indicating that his seeming fitness was insufficient to reverse his biological age and maintain true and lasting good health.)

Adelle Davis was one of this country's best-known early nutritionists, and she contended that almost any disease could be prevented through proper diet and nutrition. In particular, she emphasized the importance of eating unprocessed foods, avoiding hydrogenated and saturated fats and excess sugar, and taking vitamin supplements to guard against deficiencies. She was also an exercise advocate. Her recommendations have remained standard nutritional/fitness guidelines even as of this writing, and yet Davis succumbed to cancer in 1974 at the age of 70.[12] (Adelle Davis's life span was 50 years shorter than the God-promised 120 years, indicating that her seeming fitness was insufficient to reverse her biological age and maintain true and lasting good health.)

Bob Delmonteque—known to fans and followers as "Doctor Bob"—was a popular bodybuilder and a fitness trainer among the stars and celebrities in Hollywood. He maintained his own chiseled physique throughout his lifetime, dying in 2011 at the age of 85.[13] (Bob Delmonteque's life span was 35 years shorter than the God-promised 120 years, indicating that his seeming fitness was insufficient to reverse his biological age and maintain true and lasting good health.)

James (Jimmy) Fixx seemed to be a paragon of fitness in the 1970s. Often credited with starting the American running craze, Fixx was a vocal proponent of running and jogging in order to remain fit and attain better health. He himself ran 10 miles a day, in addition to performing other types of vigorous exercise. Friends described him as being in fine physical condition. Nevertheless, he had a fatal heart attack in 1984 at the age of 52 while jogging near his home in Vermont.[14] (James Fixx's life span was 68 years shorter than the God-promised 120 years, indicating that his seeming fitness was insufficient to reverse his biological age and maintain true and lasting good health.)

Robert Kowalski was another health guru, and he focused on the dangers of high cholesterol. His *New 8-Week Cholesterol Cure* was a *New York Times* bestseller for 115 weeks. Although "everyone" might have read his books, he still died at the age of 65 (in 2007). The cause of death was a pulmonary embolism; keep in mind he was age 35 when he had his first heart attack and bypass surgery.[15] (Robert Kowalski's life span was 55 years shorter than the God-promised 120 years, indicating that his seeming fitness was insufficient to reverse his biological age and maintain true and lasting good health.)

Dr. Michel Montignac developed the famous Montignac Diet to help himself lose weight. He was renowned both in his native France and all over the world. His research focused on the glycemic index, and the distinction between good and bad carbohydrates. (For example, whole grains were "good"; refined [white] flour was "bad.") Montignac's book, *Eat Yourself Slim,* sold 17 million copies. His theories were the inspiration behind the South Beach Diet. In 2010, Montignac died of prostate cancer at the age of 66.[16] (Incidentally, this proves that a low-glycemic diet cannot prevent cancer, itself a sign of low immunity.)

(Michel Montignac's life span was 54 years shorter than the God-promised 120 years, indicating that his seeming fitness was insufficient to reverse his biological age and maintain true and lasting good health.)

Nathan Pritikin was another well-known health guru. (His *Pritikin Program for Diet and Exercise,* coauthored with science writer Patrick M. McGrady, Jr., was quite popular, as were his health centers.) An inventor with a passion for nutrition and fitness, Pritikin was one of the first to promote the connection between diet and heart disease. Although his diet and exercise regimens enabled him to achieve excellent cardiovascular health, they were not enough to combat the leukemia that later ravaged his body. He committed suicide in his hospital bed at the age of 69 (in 1985). Some said the cancer could have established itself in his body before he formulated his diet and exercise program.[17] That might be true; however, it would only prove his program's inadequacy vis-à-vis achieving longevity, as cancer is still one of the most common causes of death! (Nathan Pritikin's life span was 51 years shorter than the God-promised 120 years, indicating that his seeming fitness was insufficient to reverse his biological age and maintain true and lasting good health.)

Dr. Roy Lee Walford, a pioneer in the field of caloric restriction, was credited with discovering that laboratory mice almost doubled their expected life spans when fed a diet that restricted their caloric intake by 50 percent. Nevertheless, he himself died at the age of 79 (in 2004). The cause of death was respiratory failure as a complication of amyotrophic lateral sclerosis (ALS, also known as Lou Gehrig's disease), an autoimmune disorder.[18] It is interesting and important to note that immune-system impairment has long been associated with calorie-restricted diets. (Roy Lee Walford's life span was 41 years shorter than the God-promised 120 years, indicating that his seeming fitness was insufficient to reverse his biological age and maintain true and lasting good health.)

Suffice it to say that advocating for fitness through exercise, good diet/nutrition, and even caloric restriction did not save any of these health experts from dying before the age of 100.˙ Not one of them attained the God-promised age of 120. The reason for this? In my professional medical opinion, it is simply that they all missed checking their telomere lengths and regularly maintaining their hormone levels.

In other words, the above examples of so-called fitness and health gurus serve to illustrate that *all* the components of a wellness/longevity program must work together synergistically: proper diet, regular exercise, and total hormone/nutrient supplementation/replacement therapy. Remember, supplementation, not substitution; we add in order to replenish the hormone levels that have been depleted from the optimum over time, but we never subtract the necessities of diet and exercise.

[**NOTE:** *Although a comprehensive exercise recommendation is beyond the scope and intention of this book, a healthy regimen of regular exercise usually consists of 30 minutes of moderate aerobic activity 2 to 3 times a week; this could include walking, swimming, water aerobics, or any other regimen approved by an individual's physician.*]

> Never subtract proper diet and regular exercise from a health regimen! Simply add to them with medically monitored supplementation.

˙ Certainly there are many other experts in the fields of health, fitness, diet, and exercise—both self-proclaimed and acknowledged within the profession—but discussing more than the number mentioned here would be beyond the scope of this book.

Maintaining the Delicate Balance—Strength, Wellness, and Resiliency

Yes, it's all about balance. The body is designed to be in balance. The problem is that humans cannot and will not ever be as wise as God, the creator of the perfect balance system of the human body. However, as we've seen throughout this book, we have the intellectual capability—and now the scientific knowledge and medical technology—to re-create and maintain that balance.

That is precisely what the total hormone supplementation/ balance therapy program is all about: achieving and maintaining balance. Optimal hormone levels lead to total balance of all body systems. This is *homeostasis,* when every system in the body is functioning optimally (see chapter 5), resulting in overall good health and well-being across the life span, even to 120 . . . and beyond.

By using the program, individuals can, and do, reverse their biological age—minimizing and even eliminating the diseases and infirmities of so-called "old age"—embarking upon attainment of the full life span with attendant good health, vibrancy, and vitality. Just as I plan to do myself! Remember, as described in the preface, I am chronologically 61, but, biologically, I am only 33.9. I therefore expect to eventually reach the biological age of 61, but that will be many chronological years from now.

> The number of years we reverse our biological age represents the minimum number of years that we have extended our life span.

To sum up, proper diet and nutrition, along with optimal hormone levels, lead to achieving body balance. It is this balance that enables strength, resiliency, and total wellness—all critical components of longevity. Once we know our own individual numbers, based on the tests described in chapters 3 and 5, we can truly embark on a program for attaining the full life span in continual good health.

In the next chapter, we will outline the steps for obtaining the tests, charting progress, and monitoring the results with a medical professional.

7

KNOW YOUR OWN NUMBERS—TESTS NEEDED TO CHECK HORMONE LEVELS AND ASSESS HEALTH

Rejoice in all the many wonderful new advances in health and healing that we humans have created.

—Louise L. Hay

Overview

Throughout the previous chapters of this book, we have discussed telomeres, telomerase, hormones, and biological health, as well as the need to create balance throughout the body by means of proper nutrition, regular exercise, and hormone/ nutrition supplementation. Armed with a solid understanding of all these, it is now time to turn our attention to the actual tests each individual needs to undergo in order to adequately check hormone levels and assess overall health. Consequently, we will review how these tests are performed, what to expect during the procedures, how to track the results, and so forth.

The goal of this chapter is to present a practical guide to the recommended tests utilized in preparation for embarking on the total hormone supplementation/replacement therapy program. Accordingly, this chapter also includes an example health log of an individual on the total hormone supplementation/replacement therapy program for longer than a year. Remember that it is essential for each of us to track and monitor our own health progress, coordinating that data with our respective physicians.*

> We each must track and monitor our own health progress (working with our physician, of course).

Tests Needed to Check Overall Health and Hormone Levels—Women

IGF-1 and IGF Binding Protein-3 (insulin growth factor)
Free T3 (*not* T3 uptake), **Free T4, TSH** (thyroid stimulating hormone)   (thyroid hormones)
DHEA (dehydro-epiandosterone) *or* **DHEA Sulfate**   (adrenal hormones)
Morning Cortisol or 4 Measurements throughout 24 hours   (adrenal hormone)
Pregnenolone   (adrenal hormone made for the maintenance of nerves and brain)
Total Testosterone *and* **Free Testosterone**   (male and female sex hormone)

---

* Throughout this book, descriptions of hormone replenishment/ supplementation therapy and diet/nutrition supplementation refer to therapies and modalities administered by a medical professional, and accompanied by appropriate monitoring on a regular basis. The information, ideas, and suggestions in this book are not intended as a substitute for professional medical advice or professional mental health advice. Before following any suggestions contained in this book, you should consult your personal physician and/or personal mental health professional.

Estradiol (E2) (estrogen) (female sex hormone)
Progesterone (female sex hormone; test best taken on day 20 to 23 of cycle for premenopausal women)
FSH (follicle stimulating hormone) (female sex hormone)
Fasting Insulin (peptide hormone)
CRP (C-Reactive Protein or Cold-Reactive Protein) (blood protein)
Serum Vitamin D Level
Chemistry 24 (blood panel including the three tests below)
- **Fasting Glucose**
- **Lipids**
- **Liver Enzymes**
CBC (complete blood count) with Differential
Complete Urinalysis with Microscopic Examination and Counts of Cells (morning awaking urine specimen)
8-Hour Collection of Urine for Environmental Chemical Toxins
Toxic Heavy Metals Screening Hair Test (by Genova)
Morning Awaking Oral Temperature by Mercury-like Thermometer or Welch-Allyn Digital Thermometer (*not* other digital thermometers)
Afternoon (between 1 and 4 p.m.) Oral Temperature by Mercury-like Thermometer or Welch-Allyn Digital Thermometer (*not* other digital thermometers)

H-Scan ("Age Scan")
(a performance test of biological age, determined by functions of various body systems, such as auditory and visual reaction times, pulmonary functions, speed of motor functions, memory, etc.)
<u>OPTIONAL</u>:
Telomere Length Test
(test of biological age, determined by length of telomeres in the DNA [by Life Length Inc.])

[**AUTHOR'S NOTE:** *If you are interested in the recommended protocol(s) described throughout this chapter but are unable to obtain a prescription for these tests from your own physician, you can obtain a complimentary prescription (doctor's order) by e-mailing me at edmundchein@yahoo.com or check.your. hormones@gmail.com.*]

Tests Needed to Check Overall Health and Hormone Levels—Men

IGF-1 and IGF Binding Protein-3 (insulin growth factor)
Free T3 (*not* T3 uptake), **Free T4, TSH** (thyroid stimulating hormone) (thyroid hormones)
DHEA (dehydro-epiandosterone) *or* **DHEA Sulfate** (adrenal hormones)
Morning Cortisol or 4 Measurements throughout 24 hours (adrenal hormone)
Pregnenolone (adrenal hormone made for the maintenance of nerves and brain)

Total Testosterone *and* **Free Testosterone** (male and female sex hormone)
PSA (prostate-specific antigen) (glycoprotein enzyme)
Fasting Insulin (peptide hormone)
CRP (C-Reactive Protein or Cold-Reactive Protein) (blood protein)
Serum Vitamin D Level
Chemistry 24 (blood panel including the three tests below)
- **Fasting Glucose**
- **Lipids**
- **Liver Enzymes**
CBC (complete blood count) with Differential
Complete Urinalysis with Microscopic Examination and Counts of Cells (morning awaking urine specimen)
8-Hour Collection of Urine for Environmental Chemical Toxins
Toxic Heavy Metals Screening Hair Test (by Genova)
Morning Awaking Oral Temperature by Mercury-like Thermometer or Welch-Allyn Digital Thermometer (*not* other digital thermometers)
Afternoon (between 1 and 4 p.m.) Oral Temperature by Mercury-like Thermometer or Welch-Allyn Digital Thermometer (*not* other digital thermometers)
H-Scan ("Age Scan") (a performance test of biological age, determined by functions of various body systems, such as auditory and visual reaction times, pulmonary functions, speed of motor functions, memory, etc.)

OPTIONAL:
Telomere Length Test (test of biological age, determined by length of telomeres in the DNA [by Life Length Inc.])

[AUTHOR'S NOTE: *If you are interested in the recommended protocol(s) described throughout this chapter but are unable to obtain a prescription for these tests from your own physician, you can obtain a complimentary test by e-mailing me at edmundchein@yahoo.com or check.your.hormones@gmail.com.*]

According to our deeper study of the above-captioned tests (see chapter 5), let's just briefly review the purpose of the recommended tests. Supplementing and replacing hormones that have fallen below optimal levels is a key method for reversing biological age and maintaining overall health and wellness. Thus, by checking hormone levels using the protocols listed above, we can assess general health. Armed with each patient's individual health information as determined by the data gleaned from these comprehensive tests, medical professionals can then create a plan tailored to that person's needs.

Let's reemphasize that all the tests listed in this chapter are extremely important for patients to have, as the results of these tests provide key information for developing a comprehensive protocol for overall wellness. Again, once all the hormone levels are optimal, the body will be in balance, and then the individual can attain and maintain good health. The ultimate goal is to achieve the full life span with attendant vitality and total well-being.

[NOTE: *Throughout this book, descriptions of hormone replenishment/supplementation therapy and diet/nutrition supplementation refer to therapies and modalities administered by a medical professional, and accompanied by appropriate* *monitoring on a regular basis. The information, ideas, and suggestions in this book are not intended as a substitute for professional medical advice or professional mental health advice. Before following any suggestions contained in this book, you should consult your personal physician and/or personal mental health professional.*]

> Optimal hormone levels and balance of all body systems lead to good health throughout the life span: living longer and with increased vitality.

What to Expect During the Testing Phase

As described when explaining the tests performed for the total hormone supplementation/replacement therapy program and for telomere-length assessment by Life Length Inc. (see chapter 5),[1] most of the analyses are completed by means of simple blood draws and/or urine specimen collections. From the patient's perspective, the procedures are no different from those performed in a physician's office or standard medical laboratory. Basically, anyone who has ever had a blood test or given a urine specimen already knows what to expect during the procedure.

The difference lies in the medical analysis of the results, not in the medical procedures used. The medical technology used to analyze the specimens collected is what enables the methods and modalities of the recommended total hormone supplementation/ replacement therapy program (see chapters 3 and 5).

> The difference between standard medical labs and those used in the total hormone supplementation/ replacement therapy program lies in the medical technology used to analyze those results, not in the medical procedures used.

What to Expect While on the Program*

Although the total hormone supplementation/replacement therapy program is designed to reverse biological age, increase longevity, and maintain overall health/wellness, every person is unique, and so individual results can—and will—vary. However, program participants do consistently live longer and in better health, reversing their biological age by means of commitment to the program and its suggestions (see examples in chapter 3).

Following a healthy regimen of proper diet and regular exercise, in addition to the supplementation of hormones and nutrients, is also key to success, as we discussed in chapter 6.

Also key to success is tracking and monitoring individual progress. That means each patient should be responsible for reviewing individual results in coordination with a trained physician. To facilitate that process, we have included an example health log. (Modify the example health log to fit your needs, and then keep it updated. Be sure to discuss your progress with your physician, obtaining clear answers to any and all of your questions.)

Follow a healthy regimen of proper diet and regular exercise, work with a physician to supplement hormones and nutrients to

---

*   Program refers to the total hormone supplementation/replacement therapy program. Examples presented are not necessarily typical, and individual results may vary. Throughout this book, descriptions of hormone replenishment/supplementation therapy and diet/nutrition supplementation refer to therapies and modalities administered by a medical professional, and accompanied by appropriate monitoring on a regular basis. The information, ideas, and suggestions in this book are not intended as a substitute for professional medical advice or professional mental health advice. Before following any suggestions contained in this book, you should consult your personal physician and/or personal mental health professional.

optimal levels, and track and monitor progress (in coordination with a physician).

Example Health Log

DIET REGIMEN	
Breakfast	½ cup cooked quinoa
Lunch	¼ pound lean turkey breast, lettuce, tomato, on whole-wheat bread
Dinner	6-ounces broiled wild-caught salmon, ½ cup cooked brown rice, 6 asparagus spears
Snacks	12 almonds and 12 bing cherries
Beverages	8 glasses (8 oz.) of water throughout day 2 mugs (12 oz.) green tea (8 a.m. and 3 p.m.)
EXERCISE REGIMEN	
Morning	Tai Chi (1 hour)
Afternoon	Bike Ride (30 minutes)
Evening	Walk (30 minutes)
TEST RESULTS	**INDIVIDUAL ON PROGRAM FOR >1 YEAR**
IGF-1 and IGF-1 Binding Protein-3	>200 µg/ml
Free T3 (*not* T3 uptake), Free T4, TSH	>25 µg/ml
DHEA *or* DHEA Sulfate	>250 µg/ml
Morning Cortisol or 4 Measurements throughout 24 hours	>15 µg/ml in AM; normal 24-hour pattern
Pregnenolone	>100 µg/ml
Total Testosterone *and* Free Testosterone	>20 µg/ml >600 µg/ml
Fasting Insulin	<25 µg/ml
CRP	<1

Serum Vitamin D Level	>80
Chemistry 24	Normal values
- Fasting Glucose	- Normal range
- Lipids	- Normal range
- Liver Enzymes	- Normal range
CBC with Differential	Normal range
Complete Urinalysis with Microscopic Examination and Counts of Cells (morning awaking urine specimen)	Normal range
8-Hour Collection of Urine for Environmental Chemical Toxins	None detected
Toxic Heavy Metals Screening by Urine or Hair	None detected
Morning Awaking Oral Temperature by Mercury-like Thermometer or Welch-Allyn Digital Thermometer (*not* other digital thermometers)	>97.6º F
Afternoon (between 1 and 4 p.m.) Oral Temperature by Mercury-like Thermometer or Welch-Allyn Digital Thermometer (*not* other digital thermometers)	>98.3º F
H-Scan ("Age Scan")	Biological age younger than chronological age
Biological-Age Determination Test (measured by telomere length [by Life Length Inc.])	Biological age younger than chronological age
	Woman on Program for >1 Year
Estradiol (E2) (estrogen)	Normal range for premenopausal woman; >100 µg/ml for postmenopausal woman
Progesterone (on 20-13 day of cycle for premenopausal women)	Normal range for premenopausal woman; >10 µg/ml for postmenopausal woman

FSH	Normal range for premenopausal woman; <15 for postmenopausal woman
	Man on Program for >1 Year
PSA	<4 for man of any age

> We are well on the way to establishing a lifelong regimen of body balance and total wellness, which will help us live longer and in better health!

We are well on the way to establishing a lifelong regimen of body balance and total wellness, which will increase longevity with attendant good health. Throughout the rest of the book, we will explore certain myths and questions related to hormone supplementation in order to show the benefits of the recommended total hormone supplementation/replacement therapy program when practiced by a trained physician (see chapter 8). We will also discuss Western medicine's resistance to certain scientific breakthroughs (see chapter 9), as well as steps we can take to safeguard our health despite environmental damages to our planet (see chapter 10).

In the next chapter, we will discuss dispelling the long-held belief that supplementation of testosterone and growth hormones can cause or aggravate cancer, as research has proved this belief to be invalid.

8

DEBUNKING THE CONTROVERSY—
TESTOSTERONE AND GROWTH HORMONE
SUPPLEMENTATION DO NOT CAUSE
OR WORSEN ANY TYPE OF CANCER

There are in fact two things, science and opinion; the
former begets knowledge, the latter ignorance.

—Hippocrates

Overview

This chapter will discuss the controversy regarding hormone supplementation as being carcinogenic, particularly as pertains to supplementation of testosterone and growth hormones. Many have long held the belief that supplementation of testosterone and growth hormone can cause or aggravate cancer, but research has proved this belief to be invalid. In fact, optimal levels of testosterone and growth hormones (as well as other key hormones and key nutrients) are necessary for maintaining body balance and overall health, and achieving the full life span with attendant well-being and vitality. (See chapters 5 and 7 for more extensive details.)

Throughout this chapter, we will present the facts and myths related to this topic, illustrating the validity of the aforementioned research.

> Optimal levels of testosterone and growth hormones are key to maintaining body balance and total wellness, and to achieving longevity.

Testosterone Supplementation—Facts versus Myths

Let's first discuss the controversy regarding testosterone supplementation; namely, whether it does or does not increase the odds of developing or exacerbating prostate cancer.

The long-held yet invalid belief that testosterone supplementation increases the odds of developing/exacerbating prostate cancer has been both disputed and scientifically refuted by Abraham Morgentaler, MD, a urologist and associate clinical professor at Harvard Medical School.[1] Any urologist who still clings to the invalid belief that supplementing testosterone increases risk of prostate cancer simply has not kept up with pertinent scientific and medical literature on the topic. Dr. Morgentaler has clearly demonstrated this in his studies on the effects of testosterone and prostate cancer, and many other medical researchers concur with his conclusions. (Dr. Morgentaler's book, *Testosterone for Life,* is highly recommended reading.)

As Dr. Morgantaler succinctly stated:

> There is not now, nor has there ever been, a scientific basis for the wrongful belief that testosterone causes prostate cancer to grow. However, there appears to be a paradox which led

urologists down this wrongful path of belief . . . . It is known that castration causes metastatic prostate cancer to regress. This, however, does *not* prove causation. This can be best explained by a saturation model. According to studies, it takes a testosterone level of 90 (reference range 200-1,100) to saturate the receptors that can accelerate the prostate cancer growth. A hypogonadal man with a testosterone level of 200 is already saturated. Treating his hypogonadism and raising his level to 800 would *not,* as multiple studies have shown, further impact the prostate cancer cells to grow.[2]

Thus, we can see from the research and conclusions drawn thereof there is no association between testosterone supplementation and increased development or exacerbation of prostate cancer.

> Testosterone supplementation does not cause or worsen prostate cancer.

Growth Hormone (IGF and HGH) Supplementation—Facts versus Myths

Having seen the lack of validity regarding the concerns against testosterone supplementation in the preceding section, let's turn our attention to refuting the validity of similar concerns against growth hormones.

Our first examination will be of research similar to Dr. Morgantaler's, in that it also looked at prostate cancer risk. Drs. Schaefer, Friedman, and Quesenberry, all medical doctors in the Kaiser Permanente Division of Research, completed a study on links between IGF-1 and prostate cancer. Their findings echo and support Dr. Morgentaler's conclusions, although in terms of IGF-1, not testosterone.

This Kaiser Permanente group reached the following conclusion as a result of their research: "There was no association between rates of prostate cancer and serum concentrations of IGF-1. A second, separate analysis of the 45 cases and 179 age-matched controls selected from the sample of 765 men confirmed the lack of association in our data."[3]

Other research supporting the benefits of growth hormone supplementation abounds. Nevertheless, the controversy that growth hormone supplementation leads to development and/or exacerbation of cancer persists, notably in two areas:

1.   Some studies in vitro (on a culture dish), as compared to in vivo (in a live human being or in living cells) showed that some types of cancer cells (in vitro) can grow faster in the laboratory.
2.   The package inserts accompanying all growth hormones clearly states: "Do not use in malignancy."

Let's consider these items one by one.

As far as item 1 is concerned, in regard to the growth of cancer cells in vitro, the human body has anticancer genes, proteins, and hormones (such as melatonin and interleukin). In other words, the human body naturally contains more hormones than just growth hormones. Therefore, the fact that some cancer cells can grow faster in the laboratory (in vitro) cannot and should not be equated with cancer cells existing in the human body.

Growth hormone supplementation simply supplements growth hormones to optimal levels. We can ask the simple question: If an individual did not have cancer at age 20, why would he or she get cancer at age 60, when the growth hormone levels were replenished to those of a healthy 20-year-old? To look at this question another way, which group has a higher level of growth hormones in their bodies, 20-year-olds or 60-year-olds? The answer is, obviously, 20-year-olds. That said, if higher levels of growth hormones cause cancer, why don't we see more cancer among 20-year-olds? Again, an obvious answer: because higher levels of growth hormones do not cause cancer. Optimal levels of growth hormones reverse biological age and promote total health and wellness.

The third point to consider in reference to item 1 is that many scientific studies have shown that growth hormone supplementation does not cause cancer, even in instances of supplementation over periods of many years. I have been on the total hormone supplementation/replacement therapy program for many years—including supplementation of growth hormone for more than 20 years—and I have not contracted any type of cancer. Again, the studies that prove this conclusion are numerous, the most famous of which was conducted by Dr. Bengtsson and his group. The patients they studied received sustained growth hormone supplementation, and none of that supplementation was associated with cancer mortality.[4] Similarly, Drs. Vance and Mauras concluded that there is "no evidence that growth hormone supplementation affects the risk of cancer or cardiovascular diseases."[5] Other research has separately reached parallel conclusions. In one case: "Although there has been some concern about an increased risk of cancer (with growth hormone supplementation), reviews of existing and well-maintained databases of treated patients have shown this theoretical risk to be nonexistent."[6] In another case: Data from long-term studies in children with both solid tumors and hematological malignancies suggest that there is no increased risk of recurrence associated with growth hormone therapy; thus, there is "no evidence of an increase of malignancy, recurrent or de novo."[7]

That brings us to item 2. As for the labeling on growth-hormone package inserts, the Growth Hormone Research Society published a paper in the *Journal of Clinical Endocrinology* stating that there is no data to support this labeling and that current knowledge does not warrant any additional warning about cancer risk. The society further states that this line should be removed from growth-hormone package inserts because there is no evidence that growth hormone supplementation increases cancer recurrence or de novo cancer or leukemia.[8]

Other various clinical studies featured in the *Journal of Clinical Endocrinology* have reported the following separate conclusion:

> There is no data to suggest that IGF-1 and IGF BP 3 modulate cancer risk in growth hormone-treated patients. Current labeling for growth states that active malignancy is a contraindication. There are no data to support this labeling. Current knowledge does not warrant additional warning about cancer risk. No evidence that growth increases cancer recurrence or de novo cancer or leukemia.[9]

Finally, Michael Sheppard, Vice Dean at the University of Birmingham Medical School in Birmingham, UK, has wrapped it up succinctly and authoritatively: "Growth hormone therapy does *not* induce cancer."[10]

My own work and research supports the foregoing findings and conclusions of my esteemed colleagues, and I am proud to be in their number. Clearly, hormone supplementation is not a significant risk factor for causing or exacerbating cancer; clearly too optimal levels of hormones are key to living longer and in better health.

> There is no risk of cancer rightfully associated with growth hormone supplementation.

Now that we have reviewed the facts—and dispelled the myths—about the carcinogenic risks of hormone supplementation, let's turn our attention to the various health modalities available today. In the next chapter, we will explore the differences between allopathic treatments (Western evidence-based medicine) and homeopathic modalities (alternative medicine), as well as the complementary/integrative treatments that encompass both, showing how the total hormone supplementation/replacement therapy program uses cutting-edge technology to empower integrative medicine to be its most efficacious. In doing so, we will address the pressing question, "Why doesn't *my* doctor know all this?"

9

THE DIFFERENCE BETWEEN WISDOM AND KNOWLEDGE—WHAT WESTERN PHYSICIANS MAY OR MAY NOT KNOW

Knowledge is proud that he has learned so much; wisdom is humble that he knows no more.

—William Cowper

Overview

In this chapter, we will define and describe Western, holistic, and integrative (complementary) medicine as they relate to the recommended total supplementation/replacement therapy program.

Integrative medicine encompasses Western (evidence-based) medicine and alternative (holistic/homeopathic) modalities. In recent years, integrative medicine has become extremely popular because it offers patients the best of Western (allopathic) medicine and alternative modalities. The recommended total hormone supplementation/therapy program endows integrative medicine with even more scientific power by means of the cutting-edge medical technology that enables the modality. By combining science, medical technology, and respect for body wisdom, we can attain the full life span while enjoying continued good health.

> Combining science, medical technology, and respect for body wisdom leads to total body balance, overall wellness, and a longer, healthier life.

Knowledge: The Benefits and Limitations of Western Medicine

Clearly, Western medicine offers many benefits to patients. Without the diagnostic tools, surgeries, immunizations, and drugs provided by allopathic medicine, many people would die and suffer from diseases and conditions that are now readily treatable. The high mortality rates among people of all ages in developing nations around the world testify to these facts.

The point to understand here is not that Western medicine has no benefits but that it has limitations. After all, if Western medicine were without limits, everyone in developed countries would be in perfect health, attain the full life span, and experience none of the conditions, diseases, or infirmities of old age. Of course, this is not the case.

For the most part, this is because Western medicine is based on facts and evidence—which is the reason why its diagnostic tools, tests, surgeries, immunizations, and drugs have proved so efficacious in so many instances over the past several decades. There is no denying that it changed the course of human health, especially throughout the 20th century, eliminating countless diseases that had scourged humankind for hundreds, even thousands, of years. However, its fact—and evidence-based nature often denies the body wisdom and balance needed for enduring health and longevity without taking pharmaceutical drugs. Those blessed individuals who attain the full life span without Western medical advances are testaments to this the world over.

The solution is to neither over—or underemphasize Western medicine's benefits or its limitations; nor to do the same with alternative modalities. We simply must make optimal use of integrative medicine: using all the scientific facts and medical knowledge we have at our disposal, combining them with the invaluable body wisdom and balance essential to lasting good health and longevity, and enhancing that combination with the medical technology that enables the attainment of the full life span with enduring wellness and vitality.

> Western medicine has significant benefits, but it is not without its limitations. If it had no limitations, everyone in the West would attain the full life span in lasting good health.

Wisdom: There Is No Substitute for Treating the Body as a Whole

It bears repeating that there is no substitute for treating the body as a whole, and this is the basis for holistic medicine and alternative healing modalities. Traditional Chinese medicine (including herbal treatments and acupuncture) and Ayurvedic medicine (a traditional medical/healing system of India) both take holistic approaches, and these systems are thousands of years old. Chiropractic, acupressure, biofeedback, healing touch, and numerous other modalities offer healing methods and approaches that are alternatives to Western evidence-based methods. Such approaches display a wide array of success rates, varying from one individual to another. For example, one person may swear by chiropractic manipulation, while another will eschew it completely yet see an acupuncturist with great results.

The point here is neither to recommend nor denounce any specific alternative modality, but rather to emphasize that we each must learn to listen to our own body wisdom, trust it, and use it to achieve and perpetuate total system balance. The only way to do this with any degree of effectiveness is to use whatever modality or method that is best for the disease's cure without taking any pharmaceutical drugs for a long period of time, and to follow a proper diet, exercise regularly, and manage physical, psychological, and emotional stress.

Ideally, we each respect and follow our body wisdom but also augment it by availing ourselves of the benefits of Western medicine; that is, following the integrative approach mentioned earlier. Needless to say, the most optimal approach to achieve a long health span and life span is the recommended total hormone supplementation/replacement therapy program, which is powered by state-of-the-art medical technology and 21st-century scientific know-how, resulting in longer life and better health.

> The most optimal approach of all is the recommended total hormone supplementation/ replacement therapy program: integrative medicine powered by medical technology and science for optimal results, lasting good health, and longevity.

"Why Don't My Doctors Know All This?"

Again, the intention here is not to judge or cast aspersions on any individual physician, treatment plan, modality, or method. The intention is simply to show all the factors that contribute to why physicians may be unaware of the recommended total hormone supplementation/replacement therapy program and/or the telomere analysis procedures that enable its implementation.

Many patients ask, "Why don't my doctors know all this?" According to Kent Holtorf, MD, Medical Director of the Holtorf Medical Group Center for Hormone Imbalance, Hypothyroidism, and Fatigue, the plain truth is that most physicians and specialists do not read medical journals outside their fields of specialty, usually because the time and effort they spend running their medical practices preclude their ability to do so.[1] I concur with my colleague Dr. Holtorf on this and on many of his other observations, including the following:

> There has been significant concern by health care organizations and experts that physicians are failing to learn of new information presented in medical journals and lack the ability to translate that information into treatments for their patients. The concern is essentially that doctors erroneously rely on what they have previously been taught and don't change treatment philosophies as new information becomes available. This is especially true for endocrinological conditions, where physicians are very resistant to changing old concepts of diagnosis and treatment, despite overwhelming evidence to the contrary, because it is not what they were taught in medical school and residency.[2]

Dr. Holtorf, in agreement with Claude Lenfant, MD, Director of the National Heart, Lung, and Blood Institute, further notes that it is of "great concern that doctors continue to rely on what they learned 20 years before and are uninformed about scientific findings . . . very few physicians learn about new discoveries [via] scientific conferences and medical journals and translate this knowledge into enhanced treatments for their patients."[3] Here again, I completely concur with my colleagues Drs. Holtorf and Lenfant.

Holtorf, Lenfant, and I are in agreement again when observing how slow the medical establishment is to adopt new concepts.[4] Lenfant summarizes this succinctly:

> Given the ever-growing sophistication of our scientific knowledge and the additional new discoveries that are likely in the future, many of us harbor an uneasy, but quite realistic, suspicion that this gap between what we know about diseases and what we do to prevent and treat them will become even wider. And it is not just recent research results that are not finding their way into clinical practice; there is plenty of evidence that "old" research outcomes have been lost in translation as well.[5]

In particular, I agree with the following observation, again by Dr. Lenfant (and supported by Dr. Holtorf[6]): effective treatment by a physician entails "the combination of medical knowledge, intuition, and judgment . . . [but that] enormous amounts of new knowledge barreling down the information highway . . . are not arriving at the doorsteps of our patients."[7]

As Dr. Holtorf also observes the "breakdown in the transfer of information,"[8] this time citing William Shankle, MD, professor at the University of California, Irvine:

> Most doctors are practicing 10 to 20 years behind the available medical literature and continue to practice what they learned in medical school . . . . There is a breakdown in the transfer of information from the research to the overwhelming majority of practicing physicians. Doctors do not seek to implement new

treatments that are supported in the literature or change treatments that are not.[9]

Although the National Center for Policy Analysis and the *Annals of Internal Medicine* both have reported concerns regarding most of the medical community's inability to "translate medical therapies into practice"[10] and failure to seek "to advance their knowledge by reviewing the current literature,"[11] the lamentable trend continues. Dr. Holtorf cites and concurs with these studies, as well as with others, including reports by the *Journal of American Medical Informatics Association* and the National Institute of Medicine.[12]

Exploring the situation from a different angle, Dr. Holtorf notes that even mainstream media have reported on the topic.[13] He and I both concur with the conclusion of Sidney Smith, MD, former president of the American Heart Association, as quoted in the *Wall Street Journal* article "Too Many Patients Never Reap the Benefits of Great Research": "A large part of the problem is the real resistance of physicians . . . many of these independent-minded souls don't like being told that science knows best, and the way they've always done things is second-rate."[14]

Finally, Dr. Holtorf concludes that the American insurance industry reinforces this trend by financially rewarding the worst physicians by allowing and disallowing reimbursement for certain methods or modalities; pharmaceutical companies contribute to this too, particularly by sponsoring free conferences, dinners, and lunches that physicians attend in order to satisfy their continuing medical education (CME)[15] requirements, and to encourage them to prescribe drugs that only treat the symptoms and signs, but that do not cure the disease (resulting in a lifetime of consumption of the company's pharmaceutical product).

Sadly, I again must agree with my colleague's conclusions.

The cumulative results of most physicians' reluctance or time-constrained inability to keep abreast of medical research, combined with the pressures exerted by the insurance and pharmaceutical industries, are that typical patients in our society do not always receive optimal care. This is simply a sad reality. Therefore, patients must keep themselves informed, not be embarrassed to ask their physicians key questions about their health (whether based on listening to their body wisdom or gleaning cutting-edge information), and seek the most effective treatments available (especially those based on current science and medical technology), to cure the disease and not just to control the symptoms and signs of the disease. For example, many people blindly stay on a lifetime course of taking the drug Lipitor to "control" their elevated cholesterol. They never research for a cure for elevated cholesterol. Neither do they know that there *is* a cure for elevated cholesterol. Furthermore, they do not know that there is a selfish ulterior motive for their doctors' putting them on Lipitor-like drugs so quickly, because then the insurance (Medicare included) pays for the follow-up visits every 6 months to monitor the side effects of the this type of drug. If a doctor has 100 such patients, his or her schedule will be full 6 months from now.

Thus, there is no simple answer to the question, "Why don't my doctors know all this?" But there is a simple way to deal with it. When your doctor doesn't know, share what you've learned! Speak up—your health (and longevity) are at stake, and 120 years of vitality and total wellness are your right, as promised by God.

Most doctors do not keep up with medical literature, so patients must educate themselves and speak up. If your doctor doesn't know something you feel is important, speak up and share what you've learned.

Integrating Knowledge and Wisdom for Better Balance

Now that we recognize that every doctor doesn't necessarily keep up with the medical literature, we can acknowledge that every practitioner we visit may not know about the most effective current treatment protocols, much less be willing to use them. That is just reality, so there is no purpose denying it or pretending it doesn't exist. The best and most we can do is to be proactive about our health and the type of treatment(s) we seek.

Remember the explanations that began this chapter: Western medicine is based on knowledge (facts) and standard tests and medications, whereas holistic/alternative modalities are based on achieving balance through body wisdom. We can also think of it this way: Western medicine treats the symptom(s); alternative modalities treat the patient as a whole (holistic approach). Western tests (lab analyses, etc.) are essential diagnostic tools, and they should not be overlooked, but neither should holistic wisdom. This is the guiding principle of integrative medicine. In essence, integrative medicine practitioners believe that scientific facts/knowledge and body balance/wisdom are equally important and should be used synergistically. Generally, integrative practitioners are usually more open-minded, more willing to accept patients who are proactive about their health, and more likely to stay abreast of current medical research, literature, and so on.

Ever since the 1970s, integrative medicine has done much to improve the quality of care and potential for achieving the full life span, in addition to improving laypeople's basic understanding of human health. The total hormone supplementation/replacement therapy program takes this a step further, bringing integrative medicine fully into the 21st century. Not only do we synergistically use scientific facts/knowledge and body balance/wisdom to the benefit of each patient, we also cull data from each patient's actual DNA in order to customize a unique treatment plan designed to ensure better health and a longer life. As seen throughout previous chapters, the telomere analyses performed determine each patient's biological age, among other key health factors, allowing medical practitioners to recommend the appropriate hormone/nutrient supplementation to increase less-than-optimal levels. Remember, without hormones and nutrients at optimal levels, the body will not be in balance, and then longevity will be more difficult to attain, and good health will be more difficult to maintain.

Integrating all the key components described above into a continual system of care and well-being is essential to living longer and in better health. Body wisdom powered by science and medical technology leads to longevity with attendant enduring vitality and wellness—and that is good health and balance for the 21st century and beyond. (After all, those born from 1981 on who attain the full life span will be alive in the 22nd century!)

> Body wisdom powered by science and medical technology leads to longevity with attendant enduring vitality and wellness—and that is good health and balance for the 21st century . . . and beyond.

Now that we have a better understanding of Western medicine, alternative modalities, integrative medicine, and the reasons why our physicians might not always know about cutting-edge research and treatment protocols, let's focus on what we need to do in order to be proactive about our health. That includes safeguarding our well-being while living in the toxic environment that our planet has become. In the next chapter, we will discuss how to establish and maintain such safeguards.

10

HOW TO STAY HEALTHY LIVING ON A POISONED PLANET—THE POLLUTED ENVIRONMENT WE HAVE CREATED

You *must take responsibility for ensuring the safety of your food.*

—David Steinman
Author, *Diet for a Poisoned Planet*

Overview

This chapter will provide tips on how to stay healthy and achieve longevity despite the ecological devastation of our planet. The goal here is to illustrate the link between the environment and human health, offering recommendations for the steps everyone needs to take in order to stay healthy in the 21st-century world. Even individuals who follow the recommended total hormone supplementation/replacement therapy program, eat a proper diet, exercise regularly, and manage stress may not live to 120 (or beyond) if they do not check for the many toxic heavy metals and poisonous chemicals that we humans have created, ruining our planet and environment through industrialization and technological advancements (e.g., nuclear reactors). There are tests to measure these toxic substances in the human body, and we will describe them later on in this chapter.

To expand on the statement offered in this chapter's opening quote, we each much take responsibility for ensuring the safety of the food we eat as well as the water we drink, the air we breathe, the fabrics in the clothing we wear, the linens we use, and so on.* It's an endless list, and our planet is oversaturated with chemicals. What can we do to ensure our ongoing good health and well-being? How can we live longer and stay healthy?

> How can we live longer and stay healthy when our planet is oversaturated with chemicals?

The Risk of Heavy Metals

Heavy metals pose a serious risk to human health. There is simply no way around that. That being the case, let's determine how the heavy metals get into our bodies to begin with.

Like the mostly contaminated fish of our oceans, we cannot excrete heavy metals once they get inside our bodies. That is why there is a limit on the amount of canned tuna that is safe to consume in the course of a week. Tuna eat other fish that were exposed to mercury from industrial wastes discharged into our oceans. Mercury and other heavy metals then accumulated in their bodies. When we eat tuna, these toxic substances in their bodies enter our bodies. This is not limited to mercury alone; in

---

* The information, ideas, and suggestions in this book are not intended as a substitute for professional medical advice or professional mental health advice. Before following any suggestions contained in this book, you should consult your personal physician and/or personal mental health professional. Neither the author nor the publisher shall be liable or responsible for any loss or damage allegedly arising as a consequence of your use or application of any information or suggestions in this book.

fact, it includes other heavy metals, such as arsenic, antimony, barium, thallium, and uranium.

Arsenic, Uranium, Barium, Thallium, Antimony

In China, where pollution is much less regulated than it is in the United States (in fact, China does not regulate some environmental poisons at all), one study[1] found the general population to possess toxic levels of heavy metals in the percentages listed below, from highest to lowest:

Heavy Metal	Toxic Serum Level
Arsenic	38%
Uranium	34%
Barium	28%
Thallium	25%
Antimony	22%
Mercury	16%

As the table above indicates, the highest level of serum toxicity is arsenic, closely followed by uranium. Arsenic's topping the list is likely the result of its frequently being ingested by means of consuming rice, a longtime staple of the Chinese diet. Interestingly, mercury has the lowest level of serum toxicity, despite receiving more public press and government attention worldwide. The other heavy metals, which are just as toxic as mercury, if not more so, receive little to no attention from the media or government agencies, although there is no ready explanation for why this is the case.

The effects of heavy-metal toxicity in the human body are numerous and frightening. Heavy metals enter our body through some of the fish we eat (mercury), some of the rice we eat (arsenic), the water we drink (arsenic and uranium), and some of the fruits and vegetables we eat if the soil they are planted in is contaminated (arsenic and others). Individuals who work in or live near certain factories and manufacturing sites are also susceptible to heavy-metal toxicity (thallium and barium, components of ant and rat poisons; barium sulfate, commonly used in diagnostic X-ray procedures), and the groundwater and soil near such factories and facilities can become contaminated, as can the fish in those waters. For example, the pipe supplying drinking water to our home might have a hole in it after many years of corrosion, and toxic chemicals (such as pesticides and industrial waste) can then slip into the pipe. Boiling the water does not eliminate any heavy metals or toxic chemicals; boiling just kills germs.

Arsenic poisoning can cause neurologic dysfunction, cardiovascular diseases, hypertension (high blood pressure), anemia, and even death. Remember that arsenic can enter the body through water and/or food; it is also a common method of intentional poisoning found in many ant and rat poisons.

Uranium poisoning (measured in the tests recommended below in a biochemical rather than radiochemical format) affects the human body's metabolism of lactate, citrate, pyruvate, carbonate, and phosphate. Eventually, uranium deposits in the kidney, bone, liver, and spleen. The initial and primary symptom of uranium poisoning is chronic fatigue. Severe levels of toxicity include kidney damage and problematic hematopoeiesis (formation of blood cells) in bone marrow. Uranium in the body can also biodegrade into radon, which causes lung cancer.

Barium poisoning usually affects the functions of the nervous system, but initially displays symptoms similar to flu, which is why it is commonly misdiagnosed. Other common symptoms of barium poisoning, especially when the toxic levels are higher or have been present longer, include muscle weakness and tremors, difficulty breathing, nausea (with or without vomiting) and/or stomach upset accompanied by diarrhea, anxiety, and cardiac irregularities (abnormally high blood pressure and rapid heartbeat).

The US Environmental Protection Agency (EPA)[2] has reported that man-made sources of thallium pollution include ore-processing operations, gaseous emissions of cement factories, coal-burning power plants, and metal sewers. Approximately 60 to 70 percent of thallium production occurs in the electronics industry, with the remainder occurring in the pharmaceutical industry and in infrared-detector and glass manufacturing. Regardless of the industries responsible for the pollution, thallium is considered a human carcinogen. The symptoms of thallium poisoning can be severe. Within 48 hours of serious exposure, nausea, vomiting, and diarrhea usually occur. Within a few days, nervous system damage becomes apparent, including such symptoms as pain, loss of reflexes, convulsions, muscle wasting, headaches, numbness, dementia, psychosis, even coma. After two to three weeks of even moderate exposure, the bases of hair shafts are damaged, resulting in alopecia (hair loss). After about three weeks, heart-rhythm disturbances occur. The most distinctive effects of slow thallium poisoning are hair loss and damage to peripheral nerves (victims frequently experience the sensation of walking on hot coals).

The foregoing facts about heavy-metal toxicity in the human body were not intended to be overly scientific or sensationalistic; they were presented merely to illustrate the severity of the risks that heavy metals pose to human health. Clearly, the best thing health-conscious individuals can do is to be tested for the presence of heavy metals in their bodies.

> We each must take the necessary tests to determine the heavy-metal toxicity levels in our bodies.

Health Tests to Check Levels of Heavy Metals in Humans

The tests available to check for heavy metals in the body can be performed through analysis of samples of hair, urine, and/or blood, following the table below:

TYPE OF HEAVY-METAL TOXICITY LEVEL ANALYSIS	TIME FRAME
Hair tests	Up to 3 to 6 months prior to test
Urine tests	Up to 30 days prior to test
Blood tests	As of the moment of the test

The laboratory analyzes the samples collected (hair, urine, and/ or blood) and then issues a report of its findings. Any individual whose lab tests indicate the presence of heavy-metal toxicity (as indicated by the laboratory's predetermined range) will need to first determine the source of exposure and then eliminate that source. This is a critical step, because heavy-metal toxicity cannot be treated until the exposure source has been eliminated. Because, like the fish, we cannot eliminate the heavy metals from our bodies, the date of exposure for a particular heavy metal is difficult to determine. It might have occurred when we were 10 years old (while swimming in the river), or it might have just occurred. Only a second test, taken after undergoing chelation treatment, can prove that the exposure is current.

Heavy-Metal Poisoning Follow-up Steps

Once diagnosed with heavy-metal toxicity, follow these necessary steps immediately:

1. Get a 3-process water-filtration device for your home water source (drinking and cooking).
   - If you already have a filtration device, have it checked to make sure it is not defective, replace it, or further investigate whether the device has sufficiently removed heavy metals from the water coming into your home.
   - Remember to use filtered water when brushing your teeth and avoid swallowing water in the shower if you are not showering at home.
2. Buy a bobble water bottle and take it with you wherever you go (work, school, errands, etc.). Bobble water bottles contain a built-in filtration system that filters water as you drink.
   - Avoid drinking from public water fountains (in municipal areas, schools, and so on).
   - Bobble water bottles are available in stores and from online retailers.
3. If it seems likely that the heavy-metal contamination came from additional or alternative sources, take the necessary measures to remove those exposure sources immediately.

Remember, treatment will not be effective until the exposure sources have been eliminated, so items 1 through 3 above are critical to ensure as quickly as possible that the treatment plan be effective.

Treatment for Heavy-Metal Poisoning

Chelation

The treatment for heavy-metal toxicity is called *chelation*. Not all physicians have the requisite knowledge and training to chelate heavy metals properly, so prior to beginning treatment, it is imperative to ensure that the practitioner is capable of administering chelation efficaciously. Equally imperative is administering a posttreatment blood test to make sure that the levels of heavy metals in the body have been reduced or eliminated accordingly. If they have not, it does not mean that the chelation was ineffective. A second course of treatment is often necessary in order to reach heavy-metal deposits in nerve and fat tissues, as it is more difficult for the chelating agent to reach these areas.*

The form of chelation that I prefer for treating heavy-metal toxicity is orally administered DMSA (dimercaptosuccinic acid). The US Food and Drug Administration (FDA) has approved DMSA chelation, but it has not approved any over-the-counter (OTC) treatments and remedies for chelation.[3] However, remember the following:

- It may take two courses of treatment to eliminate all the heavy metals from the body.
- The treatment will not work unless and until all sources of exposure have been eliminated.

---

* The information, ideas, and suggestions in this book are not intended as a substitute for professional medical advice or professional mental health advice. Before following any suggestions contained in this book, you should consult your personal physician and/or personal mental health professional. Neither the author nor the publisher shall be liable or responsible for any loss or damage allegedly arising as a consequence of your use or application of any information or suggestions in this book.

- Not every physician has the requisite knowledge or training to properly and effectively remove heavy metals from the body.

> Immediately remove the sources of exposure if lab reports show heavy-metal toxicity levels in your body, and then begin DMSA chelation as soon as possible.

How Environmental Factors Impact Health and Longevity—And What to Do to Protect Ourselves

Simply stated, God does not want us to put anything into our bodies that he did not create for the purpose of our ingesting. While most heavy metals occur naturally, their release as byproducts of manufacturing and other industrial and/or technological processes are man-made. Plus, God did not create plastic bottles and containers, pesticides, cleansers, solvents, and the like—we did. The best rule of thumb is not to ingest anything with a name that's impossible pronounce, much less spell!

> Remember, toxic means poisonous! We must remove chemical toxins from our bodies as quickly as possible.

Solvents, Cleansers, Pesticides, Plastics Bottles/Containers, Detergents, and Skin/Body Care Products

Myriad chemicals pervade our environment, and it is next to impossible to avoid them if living in the "civilized" world. Solvents, cleansers, pesticides, and plastic bottles and containers—to name but a few—all contain chemicals. Even worse, so do the detergents we use to wash our clothing, linens, dishes, glassware, utensils, and pots and pans, as well as the products we use for our skin and body care (soap, shampoo, lotion, moisturizer, makeup, etc.). When plastic bottles of drinking water are heated under the sun, the chemical phthalates are released into the water.

The chemicals in these products and substances are harmful at worst and potentially harmful at best. Many such chemicals can cause autoimmune diseases and disorders, as well as cancer. For example, a recent US Department of Agriculture (USDA) study showed that, when tested, grapes and apples already available in the marketplace contained pesticides on their skins at levels higher than those permissible for human consumption.[4] We can logically conclude that these pesticide levels will apply to other fruits and to vegetables as well.

It is extremely frustrating to feel that healthy behaviors like drinking water, eating fruits and vegetables, and so on can lead us to unwitting exposure to and ingestion of harmful chemicals, and yet this is the reality of living in today's world. Therefore, it is absolutely imperative to test for environmental chemicals in the body.

Health Tests to Check Levels of Toxic Chemicals in Humans

A simple 12-hour (from midnight to morning) urine test will check for toxic chemicals in the body (this test is similar to a pregnancy test). Be sure to find a physician qualified to deal with treating chemical toxicity, and then proceed with his or her recommendations. To detoxify chemical poisons, vitamins and amino acids, along with 8 eight-ounce glasses of water a day are required. Remember, even if eating a proper diet, exercising regularly, and following the recommended total hormone supplementation/replacement therapy program, heavy-metal and environmental chemical toxicity can still occur—and immediate removal of such toxins from the body is absolutely imperative.

> We must monitor our intake of and exposure to harmful chemicals and heavy metals, removing them when necessary. Quite simply, nothing less than our health and our lives are at stake.

The Dangers of Mold and Mildew

Mold and mildew also pose a serious risk to human health. Unlike the harmful chemicals and toxic heavy metals, substances we humans have created, these organisms are ancient inhabitants of our planet; however, that does not mean that coexisting with them is safe for us. It isn't safe for us at all, as God well knows, and which he clearly addressed in Leviticus, concerning cleansing houses of mildew/mold:

The LORD said to Moses and Aaron:

"When you enter the land of Canaan, which I am giving you as your possession, and I put a spreading mildew in a house in that land, the owner of the house must go and tell the priest, 'I have seen something that looks like mildew in my house.' The priest is to order the house to be emptied before he goes in to examine the mildew, so that nothing in the house will be pronounced unclean. After this the priest is to go in and inspect the house. He is to examine the mildew on the walls, and if it has greenish or reddish depressions that appear to be deeper than the surface of the wall, the priest shall go out the doorway of the house and close it up for seven days. On the seventh day the priest shall return to inspect the house. If the mildew has spread on the walls, he is to order that the contaminated stones be torn out and thrown into an unclean place outside the town. He must have all the inside walls of the house scraped and the material that is scraped off dumped into an unclean place outside the town. Then they are to take other stones to replace these and take new clay and plaster the house.

"If the mildew reappears in the house after the stones have been torn out and the house scraped and plastered, the priest is to go and examine it and, if the mildew has spread in the house, it is a destructive mildew; the house is unclean. It must be torn down—its stones, timbers, and all the plaster—and taken out of the town to an unclean place.

"Anyone who goes into the house while it is closed up will be unclean till evening. Anyone who sleeps or eats in the house must wash his clothes.

"But if the priest comes to examine it and the mildew has not spread after the house has been plastered, he shall pronounce the house clean, because the mildew is gone. To purify the house he is to take two birds and some cedar wood, scarlet yarn, and hyssop. He shall kill one of the birds over fresh water in a clay pot. Then he is to take the cedar wood, the hyssop, the scarlet yarn, and the live bird, dip them into the blood of the dead bird and the fresh water, and sprinkle the house seven times. He shall purify the house with the bird's blood, the fresh water, the live bird, the cedar wood, the hyssop, and the scarlet yarn. Then he is to release the live bird in the open

> fields outside the town. In this way he will make atonement for the house, and it will be clean."
>
> These are the regulations for any infectious skin disease, for an itch, for mildew in clothing or in a house, and for a swelling, a rash, or a bright spot, to determine when something is clean or unclean. These are the regulations for infectious skin diseases and mildew. (Lev. 14:33-57)

As stated previously, this book is not intended to be a spiritual exegesis (although we will address the spiritual component of health and wellness). The above has been included merely to show just how long mold and mildew have negatively impacted human health—so much so that God provided clear instructions for how to eliminate them, thereby ensuring the health of our bodies and our homes. Those are environmental protection tips we can count on!

Clearly, mold is yet another toxin we need to guard against (as is mildew, its close relation). I have seen cases of lupus and rheumatoid arthritis (both autoimmune disorders) develop as a result of mold exposure. Eliminating the exposure cured these conditions in my patients, and they never recurred. Therefore, let's learn what we can about mold in order to minimize our exposure and any adverse effects.

Mold's Negative Impact on Human Health

There is always some mold (and mildew) everywhere—in the air, on many surfaces, and so on. Mold and mildew grow wherever there is moisture; this is how and why they have survived for millions of years. As a result, exposure to damp and moldy environments may cause a variety of health effects, or none at all. Some people are sensitive to molds, whereas others are not. Those sensitive to molds can experience any number of symptoms, ranging from mild discomfort to acute severity, including headaches (especially in the morning), nasal stuffiness, throat irritation, coughing or wheezing, eye irritation, skin irritation, and even autoimmune diseases such as lupus and rheumatoid arthritis (as in the patients described above). People with mold allergies may have more severe reactions, as allergies reflect extreme sensitivities. Immune-compromised individuals and people with chronic lung illnesses, such as chronic obstructive pulmonary disease (COPD) and/or asthma, may get serious infections in their lungs when they are exposed to mold. Such individuals should stay away from areas that are likely to have mold (e.g., air conditioning and ventilation ducts, attics, basements, plaster walls, the underside of carpets, upholsteries, compost piles, cut grass, and wooded areas).

In 2004, the Institute of Medicine (IOM) found that there was sufficient evidence to link indoor exposure to mold to the following: (1) upper respiratory tract symptoms (cough, wheezing, etc.) in otherwise-healthy people; (2) increased asthma symptoms in asthmatics; and (3) hypersensitivity pneumonitis in all types of individuals.[5] The IOM also found evidence linking indoor mold exposure and asthma/respiratory illness in otherwise healthy children.[6]

In 2009, the World Health Organization (WHO) issued additional guidance, the *WHO Guidelines for Indoor Air Quality: Dampness and Mold:*[7]

Mold in the Home

Mold is found both indoors and outdoors. Mold can enter the home through open doorways, windows, vents, and heating and air conditioning systems. Mold in the air outside can also attach itself to clothing, shoes, bags, and pets, and can then be carried indoors.

Mold will grow in places with a lot of moisture, such as around leaks in roofs, windows, pipes, or walls where there has been flooding. Mold grows well on paper products, cardboard, ceiling tiles, and wood products. Mold can also grow inside walls (drywall, insulation, wallboard, etc.), on the surface of walls (wallpaper, paint, paneling, etc.), on and within carpet, fabric, and upholstery.

Controlling Mold

Inside the home, the following measures will help minimize mold growth:

- controlling humidity levels (i.e., keep the environment dry)
- promptly fixing leaky roofs, windows, and pipes
- thoroughly cleaning and drying after flooding
- ventilating shower, laundry, and cooking areas

If mold is growing in the home, clean up the mold and fix the moisture problem immediately. Mold growth can be removed from hard surfaces with commercial products, soap and water, or a bleach solution of no more than a cup of bleach in a gallon of water.

Mold growth, which often looks like spots, can be many different colors and can smell musty. The rule of thumb is this: if we can see or smell mold, a health risk may be present.

There are home mold-test kits available from online retailers, such as Amazon.com. For anyone already suffering from a serious illness, such as an autoimmune disease (e.g., lupus or rheumatoid arthritis), a urine test for mycotoxins (the toxins from mold and mildew) is essential. (RealTime Laboratories in Carrolton, Texas, is the best place for such mycotoxicology testing.)

No matter what type of mold is present, remove it immediately. Large areas and some very toxic strains of mold may require a professional mold-removal service in order to do the job correctly; in addition, protective gear while cleaning will be necessary (gloves, masks, goggles, etc.).

If using bleach to clean up mold: ***never* mix bleach with ammonia or other household cleaners.** Mixing bleach with ammonia or other cleaning products will produce dangerous, toxic fumes.

If the area to be cleaned is more than 10 square feet, consult the EPA guide entitled *Mold Remediation in Schools and Commercial Buildings.*[104] Although focused on schools and commercial buildings, this document also applies to homes. This guide is available on the EPA website at http://www.epa.gov/mold/mold_ remediation.html.

MOLD PREVENTION TIPS[8]

- Keep humidity levels as low as possible (no higher than 50 percent, 24 hours a day). An air conditioner or dehumidifier will help maintain the desired level. Bear in mind that humidity levels fluctuate over the course of a day because of changes in the moisture in the air, as well as the change in air temperature, so it is necessary to check the humidity levels more than once a day.
- Home and office air ducts must be cleaned *annually* by a professional air-duct cleaning service.
- Be sure there is sufficient ventilation. Use exhaust fans that vent outside the home in the kitchen and bathroom. Make sure the clothes dryer vents outside the home too.
- Fix any leaks in the roof, walls, or plumbing, so that there is as little moisture as possible. Remember, moisture is the environment that mold and mildew need; if they find moisture, they will grow.

- Clean up and dry out all affected areas of the home thoroughly and quickly (within 24 to 48 hours) after flooding.
- Clean bathrooms with mold-killing products.
- Remove or replace carpets and upholstery that have been soaked and cannot be dried promptly.
- Consider not using carpet in rooms or areas like bathrooms or basements that may have a lot of moisture.

To learn more about preventing mold, *see* the EPA's publication *A Brief Guide to Mold, Moisture, and Your Home* at http://www.epa. gov/mold/moldguide.html.

Yes, it is a never-ending challenge to monitor our intake of and exposure to heavy metals, environmental chemicals, mold/ mildew, and other toxins, but we simply do not have a choice. Nothing less than our health, well-being, and longevity are at stake.

> It is a never-ending challenge to monitor our intake of and exposure to heavy metals, environmental chemicals, mold/mildew, and other toxins, but we simply do not have a choice. Nothing less than our health, well-being, and longevity are at stake.

Now that we have discussed avoiding environmental toxins, the last important piece of information relative to safeguarding our health and ensuring our potential for attaining the full life span, let's review the key concepts we have learned. The next section provides a cogent recap of the essential points to remember in order to live longer and in better health.

ESSENTIALS FOR HEALTH, WELLNESS, AND LONGEVITY

Listen with love to your body's messages. It is telling you all you need to know.

—Louise L. Hay

I wholeheartedly agree with Louise L. Hays's statement about listening to your body and I strive to implement it in my own life. I have always encouraged my patients to do the same, and now I encourage you, my readers, to do so as well. In truth, respect for body wisdom is the first step toward improving health and achieving the full life span.

The following is a succinct but meaningful recap of the essential points we all must remember in order to attain and maintain good health and total wellness, and to achieve the full life span with attendant strength, vitality, vibrancy, and total well-being.

Key Points to Remember

- God's promised life span for every human is 120 years (or longer; Genesis 6:3). But there's not much point to achieving the chronological age of 120 unless we maintain our good health and vitality. In order to do that, we must keep our biological age as low as possible so that when we reach the chronological age of 120, we will be far younger biologically. (See introduction and chapter 1.)

- The reason we prematurely suffer age-related diseases and die earlier than 120 is simply that we neglect our bodies, the temples God gave each of us. (See chapter 1.) Relying on your family doctor's advice may not be enough, for he or she may not be kept up to date on all advances in medicine (especially outside his or her expertise). Make sure that each pharmaceutical drug that you take is to cure the disease and not just to control the symptoms/signs of the disease.

- Much research has shown that the control of telomere length has the potential to treat many diseases associated with aging, thereby allowing humans to appear physiologically/biologically young, to attain the God-promised age of 120, and to live beyond the observed maximum human life span of 120 years. (See chapter 1.)

- Telomeres become shorter as we age. Therefore, lengthening our telomeres is the most effective way to live longer and in better health. The best way to lengthen telomeres is to activate telomerase, the enzyme that maintains and repairs them. (See chapters 1 and 2.)

- A high percentage of short telomeres in an individual's cells will result in premature aging, disease (particularly age-related disease—that is, diseases that you did not have when you were young), and failure to attain the full life span. (See chapters 1 and 2.)

- The recommended total hormone supplementation/ replacement therapy program is designed to replenish depleted hormones in the body to their optimal levels. The end goal of this therapy is to improve health and attain the promised life span of 120—and even beyond it. (See chapter 2.)

- Measurement of biological age, which offers a view of overall health and the speed of aging, is best done by calculating the percentage of short telomeres in the DNA of your cells, expressed in "the percentage of short telomeres" in a pool of cells (the lesser the percentage, the younger the person). Thus, we can think of telomeres as cellular measures by which we can determine the difference between biological and chronological age for any and every human. (See chapter 3.)

- Time and time again, among all patients and groups studied, the data illustrates that individuals with a greater amount of optimal-length telomeres live longer and enjoy lasting good health. (See chapter 3.)

- The total hormone supplementation/replacement therapy program uses only bioidentical hormones, meaning that they are the same as the hormones created within our body. Balance, not "the more the better," is key to good health and long life. (See chapter 5.)

- Again, biological age provides a window into human health. Knowing our biological age allows us to obtain a better understanding of how diseases, lifestyle choices, behaviors, habits, and the environment all impact aging. Once we know our own data, so to speak, we have the opportunity to make appropriate changes—that is, the ones necessary to cultivate and maintain good health and to attain the full life span. Then, after making those necessary changes, we can periodically retest our DNA (but make sure that the telomeres are lengthened by the methods recommended throughout this book). (See chapter 5.)

- Telomere analysis refers to the full system of measuring each individual's telomeres and calculating the percentage of short telomeres. That analysis allows medical professionals to evaluate what antiaging or longevity program is working (or not) and to recommend changes to the program if necessary.

- Telomere length provides information about the individual's biological age, which enables medical professionals to develop a good picture of his or her overall health, rate of aging, and evidence of premature aging (if any).

- Following the initial TAT (Life Length Inc.'s Telomere Analysis Technology) procedures, patients should be tested annually in order to monitor telomere length and short-telomere percentages. (See chapter 5.)

- Patients with a large percentage of critically short telomeres should repeat the tests every six months to see if the steps they have taken to improve their biological age are working or not.

- Regular accurate monitoring of telomere length enables physicians to detect additional medical problems that were missed and to alter or add to the patients' individual customized plans/protocols as needed, based on any changes in telomere length detected in the tests. (See chapter 5.)

- Customization of the total hormone supplementation/ replacement therapy plan is crucial to design, as its intention is to allow the individual to achieve body balance and lasting health throughout the life span. (See chapter 5.)

- Hormone supplementation is an important component of any protocol designed to lengthen short telomeres. However, nutrients play a crucial role too. This means proper nutrition through a healthy diet, as well as nutrient supplementation.* (See chapter 6.)

---

* Although a comprehensive diet recommendation is beyond the scope and intention of this book, a healthy diet mainly consists of eating plenty of fruits and vegetables, whole grains, moderate amounts of lean protein, and small amounts of polyunsaturated

- Hormone and nutrient supplementation is an enhancement of a healthy regimen of proper diet and regular exercise.* Even when supplementation is used to replenish depleted hormone and nutrient levels, it is always done in addition to diet and exercise, not as a substitution for them. In other words, we don't ever subtract healthy diet and exercise, we simply add to them. (See chapter 6.)

- Proper diet and nutrition and regular exercise, along with optimal hormone levels, lead to achieving body balance. It is this balance that enables strength, resiliency, and total wellness—all critical components of longevity. (See chapter 6.)

- By checking hormone levels using the protocols described, we can assess the health condition before disease occurs, because hormones are essentially e-mails sent between organs. Armed with each patient's individual health information as determined by the data gleaned from these comprehensive tests, medical professionals can then create a plan tailored to that person's needs. (See chapter 7.)

- Although the total hormone supplementation/ replacement therapy program is designed to reverse biological age, increase longevity, and maintain

---

fats. Sugar and salt intake should be limited. The following items should be avoided: trans fats, monounsaturated fats, high-fructose corn syrup, preservatives, and artificial sweeteners, flavoring, and coloring. Individuals should consult their physicians to obtain appropriate specific dietary regimens, including appropriate intake of fiber, fluids, sugars, and sodium, as various conditions mandate different amounts of these.]

* Although a comprehensive exercise recommendation is beyond the scope and intention of this book, a healthy regimen of regular exercise usually consists of 30 minutes of moderate aerobic activity 3 times a week; this could include walking, swimming, water aerobics, or any other regimen approved by an individual's physician.

overall health/wellness, every person is unique, and so individual results can—and will—vary. However, program participants do consistently live longer and in better health, reversing their biological age by means of commitment to the program and its suggestions. (See chapters 3, 5, and 7.)

- Supplementation of growth hormones and testosterone do *not* cause or aggravate cancer. It is a long-held belief that supplementation of these hormones is carcinogenic, but studies have proved this belief to be invalid. (See chapter 8.)

- Integrative medicine encompasses Western medicine and alternative modalities. In recent years, integrative medicine has become extremely popular because it offers patients the best of allopathic medicine and alternative modalities. (See chapter 9.)

- The recommended total hormone supplementation/therapy program endows integrative medicine with even more scientific power by means of the cutting-edge medical technology that enables the modality. By combining science, medical technology, and respect for body wisdom, we can attain the full life span while enjoying continued good health. (See chapter 9.)

- The solution is to neither over- or underemphasize Western medicine's benefits or its limitations, nor to do the same with alternative modalities. We simply must make optimal use of integrative medicine: using all the scientific and knowledge we have at our disposal, combining it with the invaluable body wisdom and balance essential to lasting good health and longevity, and enhancing that combination with the medical technology that enables the attainment of the full life span with enduring wellness and vitality. (That is, the total hormone supplementation/replacement therapy program.) (See chapter 9.)

- "Why don't my doctors know all this?" Many patients ask this question regarding cutting-edge treatment protocols like the total hormone supplementation/replacement therapy program. There is no simple answer, but there is a simple way to deal with it. When your doctor doesn't know, share what you've learned! Speak up—your health (and longevity) are at stake, and 120 years of vitality and total wellness are your right, as promised by God. (See chapter 9.) You can also simply change your doctor and go to one who has the knowledge to answer your questions or cure your disease.

- Integrating all the key components described into a continual system of care and well-being is essential to living longer and in better health. Body wisdom powered by science and medical technology leads to longevity with attendant enduring vitality and wellness—and that is good health and balance for the 21st century . . . and beyond. (See chapter 9.)

- Heavy metals and environmental toxic chemicals pose a serious risk to human health. There is simply no way around that. Even individuals who follow the recommended total hormone supplementation/ replacement therapy program, eat a proper diet, exercise regularly, and manage stress, may not live to 120 if they do not check for the many heavy metals and poisonous environmental chemicals that we humans have created, ruining our planet and environment through industrialization and technological advancements (e.g., nuclear reactors). (See chapter 10.)

- Tests for heavy metals can be performed by analyzing samples of hair, urine, and blood for long-term, short-term, and immediate presence in the body, respectively. (See chapter 10.)

- The method I recommend for treating heavy-metal toxicity is oral DMSA (dimercaptosuccinic acid). However, remember the following:
    o It may take two courses of treatment to eliminate all the heavy metals from the body.
    o The treatment will not work unless and until all sources of exposure have been eliminated.
    o Not every physician has the requisite knowledge or training to properly and effectively remove heavy metals from the body. (See chapter 10.)
- There are many environmental chemicals that can poison us through intake and exposure as well. A simple morning urine test will check for toxic chemicals in the body. (See chapter 10.)
- Yes, it is a never-ending challenge to monitor our intake of and exposure to heavy metals, environmental chemicals, molds/mildews, and other toxins, but we simply do not have a choice. Nothing less than our health, well-being, and longevity are at stake. (See chapter 10.)

[**NOTE:** *Throughout this book, descriptions of hormone replenishment/supplementation therapy and diet/nutrition supplementation refer to therapies and modalities administered by a medical professional, and accompanied by appropriate monitoring on a regular basis. The information, ideas, and suggestions in this book are not intended as a substitute for professional medical advice or professional mental health advice. Before following any suggestions contained in this book, you should consult your personal physician and/or personal mental health professional.*]

This section was merely intended to highlight the key points described and to provide easy access to find them all in one place after having read the entire book. Please follow the specific chapter sources indicated in square brackets throughout the above bullet-point list to explore those topics in greater detail.

> Live to 120—and beyond—and be in your prime the entire time!

A WORD FROM THE AUTHOR

The next page contains a pledge to God that you will take care of your temple (body).

Please review this page carefully and act on its words according to your own heart and spirit.

We wish you every blessing on your journey to total health and longevity!

—Edmund Chein, MD, JD

> Remember that the deepest truth of existence is that there is a greater power than we mere humans; acknowledging, honoring, and respecting that power is essential to enduring health and wellness because humility and gratitude open us to healing.

Do you not know that your body is a temple of the Holy Spirit, who is in you, whom you have received from God? You are not your own; you were bought at a price. Therefore honor God with your body.
—1 Corinthians 6:19-20

MY PLEDGE TO GOD

I know now that the temple of the body that God gave me is just as important to maintain as the church or temple where I go to worship every week.

I know that this temple of mine was created by God solely for me. Its DNA is so unique that it never existed before I was born, nor will another copy of the same be created in the universe in the future.

I know that when I pray, I am praying from inside this temple that God gave me.

I know this, and so I pledge to God to keep this temple of mine in excellent shape to honor God—in just as good a shape as the church or temple that I regularly visit for worship, if not better.

Without this temple, I cannot serve the purpose that God put me here on this planet to fulfill, nor can I share God's word with those around me, nor service to the communities and to the ends of the earth.

I pledge to God that I will check this temple every year with advanced tests of every kind that technology has to offer and fix any disorders or defects the tests find so that every part of this temple shall function smoothly, just like the plumbing, electrical system, pillars, and foundation of the church or temple building where I regularly worship. I shall repair this temple that God gave me without taking any man-made drugs. I shall use or take only those substances that are 100 percent identical to what God gave me at birth. I shall make total wellness—of body, mind, heart, spirit, and soul—my number-one daily priority.

I pledge to God that I will make the expenses incurred for keeping my temple in good shape a higher priority than the expenses for cosmetics, clothes, cars, homes, or anything else that I own.

I hereby dedicate the temple of my body to God.

Signed by _____ Dated _____

CONCLUSION

Throughout this book, we have seen the modern medical modalities and technology (telomerase activation and total hormone supplementation/replacement therapy program) that now allow us to reverse our biological age. We can extend our life span to at least 120, the age God promised us in Genesis 6:3. Our health and longevity are up to us (and the physicians we entrust with our care and well-being).

Remember, in order to properly balance the body, maintain good health, and attain long life, our hormones and nutrients must be optimal, at the levels of a healthy 20-year-old. Plus, hormone replenishment must be accomplished by using bioidentical hormones, not synthetic materials. Of course, the total hormone supplementation/replacement therapy program is an addition to proper diet and regular exercise. And, regrettably, because we have poisoned our own planet, even those of us on the program—who do all we can to safeguard our health and well-being—must have regular tests to check for toxicity from heavy metals and other environmental chemicals/toxins.

Longevity, health, and wellness are our birthright; God promised each of us 120 years. He intended for that life span to be one of good health, productivity, and joy! Thus, if we don't make it to 120, it is because we have neglected our bodies and our health. Our poisoned planet notwithstanding, we are more intelligent and more useful to society than any prior generation. That means God's intention for us to fulfill our purpose is even stronger, and therefore the promise to attain 120 years is that much more likely.

Any of us who believe this must also believe that we owe it to ourselves to cultivate good health and to maintain our bodies as the temples God designed.

Now that we have an understanding of the foundational science and medical technology (the modalities needed to attain better health and an increased life span), as well as the spirituality, inspiration, and motivation required for our commitment to personal health and self-care (body-mind-spirit connection), it is time to take the next step.

May this book always be your guide and resource throughout every step of the exciting adventure of cultivating and maintaining good health, attaining longevity with a sustained high quality of life, and living with the enduring positive spirit of true and complete well-being that will last throughout your life span.

REFERENCES AND RESOURCES

Websites

www.lifelength.com

www.nobelprize.org/nobel_prizes/medicine/laureates/2009

www.totalhormonegenetherapy.com

Books

Baker, Heidi. *Compelled by Love: How to Change the World through the Simple Power of Love in Action.* Lake Mary, FL: Charisma House, 2008.

Baxter, Ern. *I Almost Died.* Mobile, AL: Integrity House, 1983.

Braverman, Eric R. *Younger Brain, Sharper Mind.* New York: Rodale, 2011.

Brown, Brene. *The Gifts of Imperfection: Let Go of Who You Think You're Supposed to Be and Embrace Who You Are.* Center City, MN: Hazelden, 2010.

Chein, Edmund, and Hiroshi Demura. *Bio-Identical Hormones and Telomerase: The Nobel Prize—Winning Research into Life Extension and Health.* Bloomington, IN: iUniverse, 2010.

Friedel, Dewey. *Imagine That: Unlocking the Power of Your Imagination.* Shippensburg, PA: Destiny Image Publishers, 2006.

Friedel, Dewey. *Real Men Wear Boxer Shorts.* Shippensburg, PA: Destiny Image Publishers, 1995.

Kelly, Matthew. *The Rhythm of Life: Living Every Day with Passion and Purpose.* New York: Beacon Publishing, 2004.

Kirkwood, Kerry. *The Power of Blessing.* Shippensburg, PA: Destiny Image Publishers, 2010.

Lipton, Bruce H. *The Biology of Belief: Unleashing the Power of Consciousness, Matter, and Miracles.* Carlsbad, CA: Hay House, 2005.

Morgentaler, Abraham. *Testosterone for Life: Recharge Your Vitality, Sex Drive, Muscle Mass, and Overall Health.* New York: McGraw-Hill, 2009.

Pert, Candace B. *Everything You Need to Know to Feel Good.* Carlsbad, CA: Hay House, 2006.

Ray, James Arthur. *Harmonic Wealth: The Secret of Attracting the Life You Want.* New York: Hyperion, 2008.

Rossman, Martin. *The Worry Solution.* New York: Three Rivers Press, 2010.

Seligman, Martin E. P. *Authentic Happiness: Using the New Positive Psychology to Realize Your Potential for Lasting Fulfillment.* New York: Free Press, 2002.

Zahnd, Brian. *Unconditional? The Call of Jesus to Radical Forgiveness.* Lake Mary, FL: Charisma House, 2010.

Articles

Albrecht, B. D., et al. "Hormonal Status Modulates Circulating Stem Cells in Women." *Clinical Research Cardiology* 96, no. 5 (May 2007): 258-63.

Begley, S. "Too Many Patients Never Reap the Benefits of Great Research." *Wall Street Journal*, September 26, 2003.

Bengtsson, et al. *Journal of Clinical Endocrinology and Metabolism* 85, no. 3 (2000): 933-37.

Blasco, M., C. Harley, et al. "A Natural Product Telomerase Activator as Part of a Health Maintenance Program." *Rejuvenation Research* (February 2011): 45-56.

Blasco, M., et al., *American Journal of Clinical Nutrition* 91 (2010): 1438S-1454S.

"Bob Delmonteque Dead at Age 85!" *Iron Man Magazine* (November 29, 2011) http://www.ironmagazine.com 11/29/11.

Brouillette, S., et al. "Telomere Length, Risk of Coronary Heart Disease, and Statin Treatment in the West of Scotland Primary Prevention Study: A Nested Case-Control Study." *Lancet* 369 (2007): 107-114.

Caretta, N., et al. "Erectile Dysfunction in Aging Men: Testosterone's Role in Therapeutic Protocols." *Journal of Endocrinological Investigation* 28, no. 11, Supplemental Proceedings (2005): 108-11.

Carroll, et al. "GH-IGF-I Role in Tumorigenesis." *Journal of Clinical Endocrinology and Metabolism* 83, no. 2 (1998).

Cattaneo. *Journal of Nutrition* 139 (2009): 1273-78.

Cawthorn, et al., *American Journal of Clinical Nutrition* 89 (2009): 1857-63.

Chein, Edmund Y. M. Total Hormone Replacement Therapy. US Patent 5,855,920, filed December 13, 1996, issued January 5, 1999.

Chein, Edmund. "Clinical Experience Using a Low-Dose, High-Frequency Human Growth Hormone Treatment Regimen." *Journal of Advancement in Medicine* 2, no. 3 (1999).

Chein, Edmund. "Predicting Life Expectancy, Extending Health Span, and Reversing Biological Age: How Hormone Balancing Therapy Can Reverse the Effects of Aging" (September 19, 2012). www.totalhormonegenetherapy.com/ hgh_doctor.html.

Chein, Edmund. "Retrospective Analysis of the Effects of Low-dose, High-Frequency Human Growth Hormone on Serum Lipids and Prostate Specific Antigen." *Journal of American Aging Association* 24 (2001): 59-62.

Chein, Edmund. Unpublished study on heavy-metal pollution and human intoxication in China.

Devin, J. K., et al. "The Effects of Growth Hormone and Insulin-like Growth Factor-1 on the Aging Cardiovascular System and Its Progenitor Cells." *Current Opinion in Investigational Drugs* 9, no. 9 (Sept. 2008): 983-92.

"Earth Mother to the Foodists." *Life* (October 22, 1971) http:// books.google.com/books?id=AEAEAAAAMBAJ&pg=PA70#v =onepage&q&f=false.

Farzaneh-Far. *Journal of the American Medical Association (JAMA)* 303 (2010): 250-57.

Foresta, C., et al. "Reduced Number of Circulating Endothelial Progenitor Cells in Hypogonadal Men." *Journal of Clinical Endocrinological and Metabolism* 91, no. 11 (Nov. 2006): 4599-4602.

Friedel, Dewey and Dr. Paul Meir. *Hidden Riches in Secret Places* (unpublished paper, 2007).

Furumoto. *Life Science* 63 (1998): 935-48.

Goldstein, Richard. "Jack LaLanne, Founder of Modern Fitness Movement, Dies at 96." *New York Times* (January 23, 2011) http://www.nytimes.com/2011/01/24/sports/24lalanne.html?_r=0.

Hevesi, Dennis. "Michel Montignac, Creator of Trend-Setting Diet, Dies at 66." (August 26, 2010) http://www.nytimes.com/2010/08/27/business/27montignac.html.

Holtorf, Kent. "Why Doesn't My Doctor Know This?" (April 9, 2007) http://www.prohealth.com/library/showarticle.cfm?libid=12717.

Institute of Medicine (IOM) findings on mold exposure: www.cdc.gov/mold/pdfs/findings_Institute_of_Medicine.doc.

Kang. *Aging Cell* 5 (2006): 423-36.

Kaszubowska. *Journal of Physiology and Pharmacology* 9 (December 2008): 169-86.

Lee, Y. K., et al. "Triiodothyronine Promotes Cardiac Differentiation and Maturation of Embryonic Stem Cells via the Classical Genomic Pathway." *Molecular Endocrinology* 24, no. 9 (Sept. 2010): 1728-36.

Lenfant, C. "Clinical Research to Clinical Practice—Lost in Translation." *New England Journal of Medicine* 349 (2003) 868-74.

Martin, Douglas. "Dr. Robert C. Atkins, Author of Controversial but Best-Selling Diet Books, Is Dead at 72." *New York Times* (April 18, 2003) http://www.nytimes.com/2003/04/18/ nyregion/dr-robert-c-atkins-author-controversial-but-best-selling-diet-books-dead-72.html.

"Medical Journalist and Best-Selling Author Robert E. Kowalski Remembered" http://www.npicenter.com/anm/templates/ newsATemp.aspx?articleid=19959&zoneid=2.

Mishra, A., et al. "Treatment of Chronic Elbow Tendinosis with Buffered Platelet-Rich Plasma," *American Journal of Sports Medicine* (May 2006): 1-5.

"Nathan Pritikin Biography" OAC/UCLA Document Archive (content-backend-a.cdlib.org/view?docID=kt6h4nc7rg&chunk. id=bioghist-1.83&brand=oac).

National Center for Policy Analysis. "Science Knows Best." *Daily Project Digest* (September 26, 2003).

Nemoto. *Biochemical Pharmacology* 59 (2000): 401-405.

Niteesh, C., et al. "Systematic Review: The Relationship between Clinical Experience and Quality of Health Care." *Annals of Internal Medicine* (February 15, 2005).

Richards. *American Journal of Clinical Nutrition* 86 (2007): 1420-25.

"Roy Lee Walford, MD, Biography" http://www.walford.com/bio. htm.

Sanchez, G. *Journal of Endocrinology* 185 (June 2005): 421-28.

Schaefer, Friedman, and Quesenberry. *IGF-1 and Prostate Cancer.* Medical research study, Kaiser Permanente Division of Research.

Schernhammer, et al. "IGF-1 and HG Levels Were Not Associated with Breast Cancer Risk." *The Nurses' Health Study II, Endocrine Related Cancer* 13, no. 2 (June 2006): 583-92.

Shankle, William. Keynote Presentation. International Conference on the Integrative Medical Approach to the Prevention of Alzheimer's Disease (October 11, 2003).

Shay, J., W. Wright, and C. Harley. "Telomeres and Telomerase: From Discovery to Clinical Trials" http://www.ncbi.nlm.nih. gov/pmc/articles/PMC2810624/.

Sheppard, M. "Growth Hormone Therapy Does Not Induce Cancer," *Endocrinology and Metabolism,* 2, no. 10 (October 2005). (Michael Sheppard is Vice Dean, University of Birmingham Medical School, Birmingham, England, UK.)

Sheppard, M. *Endocrinology and Metabolism* 2, no. 10 (October 2005).

Sinha-Hikim, I., et al. "Effects of Testosterone Supplementation on Skeletal Muscle Fiber Hypertrophy and Satellite Cells in Community-Dwelling Older Men." *Journal of Clinical Endocrinology and Metabolism* 91, no. 8 (Aug. 2006): 3024-33.

Sun, H., et al. "Effects of Estrogen on Stem Cells and Relevant Intracellular Mechanisms." *Science China Life Sciences* (*SpringerOpen Journal*) 53, no. 5 (May 2010): 542-47.

Tanaka. *Journal of Cell Biochemistry* 102 (2007): 689-703.

The Endocrine Society. "Growth Hormone Replacement Has No Cancer Risk." *Journal of Clinical Endocrinology.*

"The Legacy of Jim Fixx" http://www.halhigdon.com/Articles/Fixx.htm.

Thum, T., et al. "Age-Dependent Impairment of Endothelial Progenitor Cells Is Corrected by Growth Hormone-Mediated Increase of Insulin-like Growth Factor-1." *Circulation Research* 100, no. 3 (Feb. 2007): 434-43.

US Department of Agriculture (USDA) *Annual Pesticide Summary,* http:www.ams.usda.gov/amsv1.0/pdp.

US Environmental Protection Agency (EPA) documents on thallium pollution and poisoning: water.epa.gov/.../contaminants/basicinformation/thallium.cfm; www.epa.gov/safewater/pdfs/factsheets/ioc/thallium.pdf.

US Environmental Protection Agency (EPA). *A Brief Guide to Mold, Moisture, and Your Home.* http://www.epa.gov/mold/moldguide.html.

US Environmental Protection Agency (EPA). *Mold Remediation in Schools and Commercial Buildings.* http://www.epa.gov/mold/mold_remediation.html.

US Food and Drug Administration (FDA) documents on DMSA chelation: www.fda.gov/downloads/NewsEvents/Newsroom/MediaTranscripts/UCM230032.pdf.

Van der Klaauw, A. A., et al. "Influence of the d3-GH Receptor Isoform on Short-Term and Long-Term Treatment Response to GH Replacement in GH-Deficient Adults." *Journal of Clinical Endocrinology and Metabolism* 93, no. 7 (July 1008): 2828.

Vance, Mary Lee, and Nelly Mauras. "Growth Hormone Therapy in Adults and Children." *New England Journal of Medicine* (October 14, 1999).

Wang, J. M., et al. "The Neurosteroid Allopregnanolone Promotes Proliferation of Rodent and Neural Progenitor Cells and Regulates Cell-Cycle Gene and Protein Expression." *Journal of Neuroscience* 25, no. 19 (May 2005): 4706-18.

Williams, K., and K. Boggess. *Journal of Clinical Endocrinology and Metabolism* 86 (August 2001): 3912-17.

World Health Organization (WHO). *WHO Guidelines for Indoor Air Quality: Dampness and Mold* (2009). http://www.who.int/indoorair/publications/7989289041683/en/.

Xu, H., et al., (in coordination with the NIH). *American Journal of Clinical Nutrition* 89 (2009): 1857-63.

Yokoo. *Journal of Cell Biochemistry* 93 (2004): 588-97.

Research Studies

Devin, J. K., et al. "Effects of Growth-Hormone Administration." Research Study. University of Texas MD Anderson Cancer Center, Department of Endocrine Neoplasia and Hormonal Disorders, Houston, TX.

Hoeber, T., et al. "IGF-1, Growth Hormone, and Stem Cells." Research Study. Universitat Wurzburg, Medizinische Klinik I (Kardiologie), Wurzburg, Germany (2007).

Mias, C. et al. "Pretreatment with Melatonin Improves Survival and Efficiency of Stem Cells Injected into Ischemic Kidney." Research Study. Institute National de la Sante de la Recherche Medicale, U858, Institut de Medecine Moleculaire de Rangueil, Toulouse, France.

Shin, S., et al. "IGF-1 Promotes Stem-Cell Growth." Research Study. Life Technologies, Frederick, MD (2010).

ABOUT EDMUND CHEIN, MD, JD

Edmund Chein, MD, JD, is a well-respected specialist in longevity medicine and telomerase activation therapy. He has restored the health and well-being of countless patients, including those disabled, traumatized, and severely ill. His patented total hormone supplementation/replacement therapy program has been recognized by colleagues throughout the medical and scientific community.

He is the founder of the American Academy of Longevity Medicine, the American Board of Longevity Medicine, the Autologous Stem Cell Therapy Institute, and the Palm Springs Life Extension Institute. He is a member of the American Medical Association (AMA), the American Academy of Anti-Aging Medicine, the American Academy of Environmental Medicine, and the California Society of Physical Medicine and Rehabilitation.

Newsweek, Health and Medicine for Physicians, and *Life Extension* magazine are but a few of the publications that have reported on Dr. Chein's groundbreaking work, and he has made countless media appearances nationwide. His publications include *Age Reversal: From Hormones to Telomerase*; *The Origin of Beauty and Youth*; *Bio-Identical Hormones and Telomerase: The Nobel Prize—Winning Research into Human Life Extension*; "Clinical Experience Using a Low-Dose, High-Frequency Human Growth Hormone Treatment Regimen"; and "Retrospective Analysis of the Effects of Low-Dose, High-Frequency Human Growth Hormone on Serum Lipids and Prostate Specific Antigen."

NOTES

1. A Long Life—God's Promise

[1] Edmund Chein and Hiroshi Demura, *Bio-Identical Hormones and Telomerase: The Nobel Prize—Winning Research into Life Extension and Health,* (Bloomington, IN: iUniverse, 2010); www.totalhormonegenetherapy.com; www.lifelength.com.

2. Telomeres and Telomerase: How They Impact Longevity and Lasting Good Health

[1] Encapsulations of Muller research: Edmund Chein and Hiroshi Demura, *Bio-Identical Hormones and Telomerase: The Nobel Prize—Winning Research into Life Extension and Health,* (Bloomington, IN: iUniverse, 2010); www.totalhormonegenetherapy.com; www.lifelength.com.

[2] Encapsulations of McClintock research, ibid.

[3] Encapsulations of Olovnikov and Watson research, ibid.

[4] Encapsulations of Blackburn and Szostak research, ibid.

[5] Encapsulations of Blackburn and Greider research, ibid.

[6] Encapsulations of Blackburn, Greider, and Szostak research, ibid.; Nobel Prize in Medicine, 2009 www.nobelprize.org/nobel_prizes/medicine/laureates/2009.

[7] Texas University Southwestern School of Medicine, various research.

[8] R. Cawthorn, et al., www.zoominfo.com/p/Richard-Cawthorn/142144719.

9   M. Blasco, et al., *American Journal of Clinical Nutrition* 91 (2010): 1438S-1454S.

10   J. Shay, W. Wright, and C. Harley, "Telomeres and Telomerase: From Discovery to Clinical Trials" http://www.ncbi.nlm.nih.gov/pmc/articles/PMC2810624/; plus various other collective research.

11   K. Williams and K. Boggess, *Journal of Clinical Endocrinology and Metabolism* 86 (August 2001): 3912-17.

12   G. Sanchez, *Journal of Endocrinology* 185 (June 2005): 421-28.

13   M. Sheppard, *Endocrinology and Metabolism* 2, no. 10 (October 2005).

14   S. *Brouillette, et al., "Telomere Length, Risk of Coronary Heart Disease, and Statin Treatment in the West of Scotland Primary Prevention Study: A Nested Case-Control Study," Lancet 369 (*2007)*: 107-114.*

15   Kaszubowska, *Journal of Physiology and Pharmacology* 9 (December 2008): 169-86.

16   Georgetown University and National Cancer Institute study, http://www.ncbi.nlm.nih.gov/pubmed/23513041

17   H. Xu, et al., (in coordination with the NIH), *American Journal of Clinical Nutrition* 89 (2009): 1857-63.

18   Encapsulations of Blackburn, Greider, and Szostak research: Edmund Chein and Hiroshi Demura, *Bio-Identical Hormones and Telomerase: The Nobel Prize—Winning Research into Life Extension and Health,* (Bloomington, IN: iUniverse, 2010); www.totalhormonegenetherapy.com; www.lifelength.com.; Nobel Prize in Medicine, 2009 www.nobelprize.org/nobel_prizes/medicine/laureates/2009.

19   Collective cancer research by international team (July 2010) www.stopthebodyclock.com/cancer--telomerase.html.

20   M. Blasco, C. Harley, et al., "A Natural Product Telomerase Activator as Part of a Health Maintenance Program," *Rejuvenation Research* (February 2011): 45-56.

[21] Edmund Y. M. Chein, Total Hormone Replacement Therapy, US Patent 5,855,920, filed December 13, 1996, issued January 5, 1999.

3. The Telomere Yardstick: Three Separate Studies of Biological Age

[1] Edmund Chein and Hiroshi Demura, *Bio-Identical Hormones and Telomerase: The Nobel Prize—Winning Research into Life Extension and Health,* (Bloomington, IN: iUniverse, 2010); www.totalhormonegenetherapy.com; www.lifelength. com.

[2] http://www.lifelength.com/technology.html.

[3] Ibid.

[4] S. *Brouillette, et al., "Telomere Length, Risk of Coronary Heart Disease, and Statin Treatment in the West of Scotland Primary Prevention Study: A Nested Case-Control Study," Lancet 369 (*2007*): 107-114.*

4. Which Bioidentical Hormones Are Related to Your Stem Cells in Regeneration and Rejuvenation?

[1] A. Mishra, et al., "Treatment of Chronic Elbow Tendinosis with Buffered Platelet-Rich Plasma," *American Journal of Sports Medicine* (May 2006): 1-5.

J. K. Devin, et al., "The Effects of Growth Hormone and Insulin-like Growth Factor-1 on the Aging Cardiovascular System and Its Progenitor Cells," *Current Opinion in Investigational Drugs* 9, no. 9 (Sept. 2008): 983-92.

T. Thum, et al., "Age-Dependent Impairment of Endothelial Progenitor Cells Is Corrected by Growth Hormone-Mediated Increase of Insulin-like Growth Factor-1," *Circulation Research* 100, no. 3 (Feb. 2007): 434-43.

N. Caretta, et al., "Erectile Dysfunction in Aging Men: Testosterone's Role in Therapeutic Protocols," *Journal of*

Endocrinological Investigation 28, no. 11, Supplemental Proceedings (2005): 108-11.

I. Sinha-Hikim, et al., "Effects of Testosterone Supplementation on Skeletal Muscle Fiber Hypertrophy and Satellite Cells in Community-Dwelling Older Men," *Journal of Clinical Endocrinology and Metabolism* 91, no. 8 (Aug. 2006): 3024-33.

C. Foresta, et al., "Reduced Number of Circulating Endothelial Progenitor Cells in Hypogonadal Men," *Journal of Clinical Endocrinological and Metabolism* 91, no. 11 (Nov. 2006): 4599-4602.

J. M. Wang, et al., "The Neurosteroid Allopregnanolone Promotes Proliferation of Rodent and Neural Progenitor Cells and Regulates Cell-Cycle Gene and Protein Expression," *Journal of Neuroscience* 25, no. 19 (May 2005): 4706-18.

[2] S. Shin, et al., "IGF-1 Promotes Stem-Cell Growth," Research Study, Life Technologies, Frederick, MD (2010).

[3] T. Hoeber, et al., "IGF-1, Growth Hormone, and Stem Cells," Research Study, Universitat Wurzburg, Medizinische Klinik I (Kardiologie), Wurzburg, Germany (2007).

[4] Ibid.

[5] Ibid.

[6] J. K. Devin, et al., "Effects of Growth-Hormone Administration," Research Study, University of Texas MD Anderson Cancer Center, Department of Endocrine Neoplasia and Hormonal Disorders, Houston, TX.

[7] Ibid.

[8] Ibid.

[9] A. A. Van der Klaauw, et al., "Influence of the d3-GH Receptor Isoform on Short-Term and Long-Term Treatment Response to GH Replacement in GH-Deficient Adults," *Journal of Clinical Endocrinology and Metabolism* 93, no. 7 (July 1008): 2828.

[10] H. Sun, et al., "Effects of Estrogen on Stem Cells and Relevant Intracellular Mechanisms," *Science China Life*

Sciences (*SpringerOpen Journal*) 53, no. 5 (May 2010): 542-47.

[11] B. D. Albrecht, et al., "Hormonal Status Modulates Circulating Stem Cells in Women," *Clinical Research Cardiology* 96, no. 5 (May 2007): 258-63.

[12] J. M. Wang, et al., "The Neurosteroid Allopregnanolone Promotes Proliferation of Rodent and Neural Progenitor Cells and Regulates Cell-Cycle Gene and Protein Expression," *Journal of Neuroscience* 25, no. 19 (May 2005): 4706-18.

[13] Y. K. Lee, et al., "Triiodothyronine Promotes Cardiac Differentiation and Maturation of Embryonic Stem Cells via the Classical Genomic Pathway," *Molecular Endocrinology* 24, no. 9 (Sept. 2010): 1728-36.

[14] C. Mias, et al., "Pretreatment with Melatonin Improves Survival and Efficiency of Stem Cells Injected into Ischemic Kidney," Research Study, Institute National de la Sante de la Recherche Medicale, U858, Institut de Medecine Moleculaire de Rangueil, Toulouse, France.

5. The Method and Medical Technology of the 21st Century—How to Reverse Biological Age, Attain Better Health, and Increase the Life Span

[1] http://www.lifelength.com/technology.html.

[2] Ibid.

[3] Edmund Chein and Hiroshi Demura, *Bio-Identical Hormones and Telomerase: The Nobel Prize—Winning Research into Life Extension and Health,* (Bloomington, IN: iUniverse, 2010); Edmund Chein, "Clinical Experience Using a Low-Dose, High-Frequency Human Growth Hormone Treatment Regimen," *Journal of Advancement in Medicine* 2, no. 3 (1999); Edmund Chein, "Retrospective Analysis of the Effects of Low-dose, High-Frequency Human Growth Hormone on Serum Lipids and Prostate Specific Antigen," *Journal of American Aging Association* 24 (2001): 59-62; www.totalhormonegenetherapy.com; www.lifelength.com.

4   Ibid; as well as Dr. Chein's various letters to patients.

5   Ibid.

6   http://www.lifelength.com/technology.html.

7   Ibid.

8   Life Length is the only company globally that can provide individuals a scientifically rigorous estimate of biological age based on the percentage of critically short telomeres measured in blood as a surrogate for the overall organism. http://www.lifelength.com/technology.html.

9   http://www.lifelength.com/technology.html.

10   Ibid.

11   Ibid.

12   Ibid.

6.   The Delicate Balance of a Strong Body—The Difference between Hormone Supplementation and Nutrition

1   Edmund Chein, "Predicting Life Expectancy, Extending Health Span, and Reversing Biological Age: How Hormone Balancing Therapy Can Reverse the Effects of Aging," (September 19, 2012), www.totalhormonegenetherapy.com/hgh_doctor.html.

2   Research on vitamin B12 and folate lengthening telomeres: Cattaneo, *Journal of Nutrition* 139 (2009): 1273-78; Xu, *American Journal of Clinical Nutrition* 89 (2009): 1857-63.

3   Research on omega-3 fatty acid: Farzaneh-Far, *Journal of the American Medical Association (JAMA)* 303 (2010): 250-57.

4   Research on vitamin C and vitamin E: Furumoto, *Life Science* 63 (1998): 935-48; Yokoo, *Journal of Cell Biochemistry* 93 (2004): 588-97; Tanaka, *Journal of Cell Biochemistry* 102 (2007): 689-703.

5   Research on nicotinamide (vitamin B3): Kang, *Aging Cell* 5 (2006): 423-36.

6   Research on zinc: Nemoto, *Biochemical Pharmacology* 59 (2000): 401-405.

[7]   Research on vitamin D: Richards, *American Journal of Clinical Nutrition* 86 (2007): 1420-25.

[8]   Research on magnesium: Xu, *American Journal of Clinical Nutrition* 89 (2009): 1857-63.

[9]   www.totalhormonegenetherapy.com; www.lifelength.com; Dr. Chein's various letters to patients.

[10]   Information on Jack LaLanne: Richard Goldstein, "Jack LaLanne, Founder of Modern Fitness Movement, Dies at 96," *New York Times* (January 23, 2011) http://www.nytimes.com/2011/01/24/sports/24lalanne.html?_r=0.

[11]   Information on Dr. Robert C. Atkins: Douglas Martin, "Dr. Robert C. Atkins, Author of Controversial but Best-Selling Diet Books, Is Dead at 72," *New York Times* (April 18, 2003) http://www.nytimes.com/2003/04/18/nyregion/dr-robert-c-atkins-author-controversial-but-best-selling-diet-books-dead-72.html.

[12]   Information on Adelle Davis: "Earth Mother to the Foodists," *Life* (October 22, 1971) http://books.google.com/books?id=AEAEAAAAMBAJ&pg=PA70#v=onepage&q&f=false.

[13]   Information on Bob Delmonteque: "Bob Delmonteque Dead at Age 85!" *Iron Man Magazine* (November 29, 2011) http://www.ironmagazine.com 11/29/11.

[14]   Information on Jim Fixx: "The Legacy of Jim Fixx" http://www.halhigdon.com/Articles/Fixx.htm.

[15]   Information on Robert E. Kowalski: "Medical Journalist and Best-Selling Author Robert E. Kowalski Remembered" http://www.npicenter.com/anm/templates/newsATemp.aspx?articleid=19959&zoneid=2.

[16]   Information on Dr. Michel Montignac: Dennis Hevesi, "Michel Montignac, Creator of Trend-Setting Diet, Dies at 66," (August 26, 2010) http://www.nytimes.com/2010/08/27/business/27montignac.html.

[17]   Information on Nathan Pritikin: "Nathan Pritikin Biography," OAC/UCLA Document Archive (content-backend-a.cdlib.org/view?docID=kt6h4nc7rg&chunk.id=bioghist-1.83&brand=oac).

[18]   Information on Dr. Roy Lee Walford: "Roy Lee Walford, MD, Biography" http://www.walford.com/bio.htm.

7.   Know Your Own Numbers—Tests Needed to Check Hormone Levels and Assess Health

[1]   Edmund Chein, "Predicting Life Expectancy, Extending Health Span, and Reversing Biological Age: How Hormone Balancing Therapy Can Reverse the Effects of Aging," (September 19, 2012), www.totalhormonegenetherapy.com/hgh_doctor.html; http://www.lifelength.com/technology.html.

8.   Debunking the Controversy—Testosterone and Growth Hormone Supplementation Do Not Cause or Worsen Any Type of Cancer

[1]   Abraham Morgentaler, *Testosterone for Life: Recharge Your Vitality, Sex Drive, Muscle Mass, and Overall Health* (New York: McGraw-Hill, 2009).

[2]   Ibid.

[3]   Drs. Schaefer, Friedman, and Quesenberry, *IGF-1 and Prostate Cancer.* Medical research study, Kaiser Permanente Division of Research.

[4]   Bengtsson, et al., *Journal of Clinical Endocrinology and Metabolism* 85, no. 3 (2000): 933-37.

[5]   Mary Lee Vance and Nelly Mauras, "Growth Hormone Therapy in Adults and Children," *New England Journal of Medicine* (October 14, 1999).

[6]   Schernhammer, et al., "IGF-1 and HG Levels Were Not Associated with Breast Cancer Risk," *The Nurses' Health Study II, Endocrine Related Cancer* 13, no. 2 (June 2006): 583-92.

[7]   Carroll, et al., "GH-IGF-I Role in Tumorigenesis," *Journal of Clinical Endocrinology and Metabolism* 83, no. 2 (1998).

[8]   The Endocrine Society, "Growth Hormone Replacement Has No Cancer Risk," *Journal of Clinical Endocrinology.*

9   Various research, *Journal of Clinical Endocrinology and Metabolism* (May 2001).

10 M. Sheppard, "Growth Hormone Therapy Does Not Induce Cancer," *Endocrinology and Metabolism,* 2, no. 10 (October 2005). (Michael Sheppard is Vice Dean, University of Birmingham Medical School, Birmingham, England, UK.)

9. The Difference between Wisdom and Knowledge—What Western Physicians May or May Not Know

1   Kent Holtorf, "Why Doesn't My Doctor Know This?" (April 9, 2007) http://www.prohealth.com/library/showarticle.cfm?libid =12717.

2   Ibid.

3   Ibid.; C. Lenfant, "Clinical Research to Clinical Practice— Lost in Translation," *New England Journal of Medicine* 349 (2003) 868-74.

4   Kent Holtorf, "Why Doesn't My Doctor Know This?" (April 9, 2007) http://www.prohealth.com/library/showarticle.cfm?libid =12717; C. Lenfant, "Clinical Research to Clinical Practice— Lost in Translation," *New England Journal of Medicine* 349 (2003): 868-74.

5   Ibid.

6   Kent Holtorf, "Why Doesn't My Doctor Know This?" (April 9, 2007) http://www.prohealth.com/library/showarticle.cfm?libid =12717.

7   C. Lenfant, "Clinical Research to Clinical Practice—Lost in Translation," *New England Journal of Medicine* 349 (2003): 868-74.

8   Kent Holtorf, "Why Doesn't My Doctor Know This?" (April 9, 2007) http://www.prohealth.com/library/showarticle.cfm?libid =12717.

9   William Shankle, Keynote Presentation, International Conference on the Integrative Medical Approach to the Prevention of Alzheimer's Disease (October 11, 2003).

[10] National Center for Policy Analysis, "Science Knows Best," *Daily Project Digest* (September 26, 2003).

[11] C. Niteesh, et al., "Systematic Review: The Relationship between Clinical Experience and Quality of Health Care," *Annals of Internal Medicine* (February 15, 2005).

[12] Kent Holtorf, "Why Doesn't My Doctor Know This?" (April 9, 2007) http://www.prohealth.com/library/showarticle.cfm?libid =12717.

[13] Ibid.

[14] S. Begley, "Too Many Patients Never Reap the Benefits of Great Research," *Wall Street Journal,* (September 26, 2003).

[15] Kent Holtorf, "Why Doesn't My Doctor Know This?" (April 9, 2007) http://www.prohealth.com/library/showarticle.cfm?libid =12717.

10. How to Stay Healthy Living on a Poisoned Planet—The Polluted Environment We Have Created

[1] Edmund Chein, unpublished study on heavy-metal pollution and human intoxication in China.

[2] US Environmental Protection Agency (EPA) documents on thallium pollution and poisoning: water.epa.gov/.../contaminants/basicinformation/thallium.cfm; www.epa.gov/safewater/pdfs/factsheets/ioc/thallium.pdf.

[3] US Food and Drug Administration (FDA) documents on DMSA chelation: www.fda.gov/downloads/NewsEvents/Newsroom/MediaTranscripts/UCM230032.pdf.

[4] US Department of Agriculture (USDA) *Annual Pesticide Summary,* http:www.ams.usda.gov/amsv1.0/pdp.

[5] Institute of Medicine (IOM) findings on mold exposure: www.cdc.gov/mold/pdfs/findings_Institute_of_Medicine.doc.

[6] Ibid.

[7] World Health Organization (WHO) *WHO Guidelines for Indoor Air Quality: Dampness and Mold,* 2009, http://www.who.int/indoorair/publications/7989289041683/en/.

[8]   US Environmental Protection Agency (EPA) *Mold Remediation in Schools and Commercial Buildings* http://www.epa.gov/mold/mold_remediation.html.

[9]   US Environmental Protection Agency (EPA) *A Brief Guide to Mold, Moisture, and Your Home* at http://www.epa.gov/mold/moldguide.html.